The Sunny S

An Autumn in Spain an

John William Clayton

Alpha Editions

This edition published in 2024

ISBN : 9789364735360

Design and Setting By
Alpha Editions
www.alphaedis.com
Email - info@alphaedis.com

As per information held with us this book is in Public Domain.
This book is a reproduction of an important historical work. Alpha Editions uses the best technology to reproduce historical work in the same manner it was first published to preserve its original nature. Any marks or number seen are left intentionally to preserve its true form.

Contents

CHAPTER I. .... - 1 -

CHAPTER II. .... - 7 -

    FOOTNOTE: .... - 14 -

CHAPTER III. .... - 15 -

    FOOTNOTE: .... - 24 -

CHAPTER IV. .... - 25 -

    FOOTNOTES: .... - 33 -

CHAPTER V. .... - 34 -

CHAPTER VI. .... - 43 -

    FOOTNOTES: .... - 50 -

CHAPTER VII. .... - 51 -

    FOOTNOTES: .... - 58 -

CHAPTER VIII. .... - 60 -

    FOOTNOTES: .... - 66 -

CHAPTER IX. .... - 67 -

FOOTNOTES: ....- 71 -

CHAPTER X. ....- 72 -

FOOTNOTES: ....- 81 -

CHAPTER XI. ....- 83 -

FOOTNOTES: ....- 92 -

CHAPTER XII. ....- 93 -

FOOTNOTES: ....- 100 -

CHAPTER XIII. ....- 101 -

FOOTNOTES: ....- 105 -

CHAPTER XIV. ....- 106 -

FOOTNOTE: ....- 112 -

CHAPTER XV. ....- 113 -

CHAPTER XVI. ....- 119 -

CHAPTER XVII. ....- 125 -

CHAPTER XVIII. ....- 132 -

CHAPTER I.

FOLLOWERS OF MAXIMILIAN OF MEXICO.—HAVRE DE GRÂCE.—ROUEN.—THE CATHEDRAL.—INFLUENCE OF SACRED MUSIC.—HEART OF RICHARD I. OF ENGLAND.—ANCIENT QUARTERS OF ROUEN.—MOUNT ST. CATHERINE.—THE SEINE.—NORMAN PEASANT GIRLS.—LISIEUX.—STOPPAGE AT MEZIDON.

IT was almost at the last moment when, after having bid farewell to all our friends, we found ourselves on board the steamer that was to take us from England on an autumn tour to the sunny south. There was great noise and bustle on deck; the friends of the departing passengers had all left the ship, and in a few minutes the anchor was weighed.

It was yet early morning, and the sun was rising with great brilliance in the east; but his appearance was only momentary, for while we were rejoicing in the prospect of a beautiful sunlit day, he suddenly withdrew from our sight, and hid his glorious visage behind a thick cloud. So unexpected was his obscuration, that we could almost have fancied he had covered his face with a veil to conceal from his sight a scene of unexampled squalor and misery that lay heaped upon the fore-deck. A band of fifty followers of the unfortunate Maximilian of Mexico, who had landed in England a day or two before, were now being wafted by a friendly breeze, not the less welcome that it came so late, towards their homes, with simply nothing left to them but their lives.

Without other clothing than a few parti-coloured rags, which but a short time back had composed the gay panoply of war, clinging to their festering bodies, without that glory which, in the lack of every other reward, is often sufficient to compensate soldiers for having left the happy hearths of their homes and the loving eyes of their kindred, these sons of fair-haired Austria were slowly returning, feeble in body and broken down in spirit, to their fatherland, carrying with them the mortifying recollection of a shameful defeat at the hands of a distant, half-barbarous race whom they had despised, and with the destruction of health for life, the loss of limbs, and the blighting of hopes which they had once nourished. Such were the subjects, such the colours, which composed this little illustrative picture of the pomp and circumstance of glorious war. Those young soldiers, all of whom were either suffering from wounds or prostrated by sickness, were standing on the deck in haggard groups, chatting about their native place, about the home of their youth, or about the plans which they intended to carry out when they arrived there. A few were groaning with pain, some of them suffering so severely as to be almost insensible to what was passing around them. Others who were in a comparatively sound condition were laughing and dancing, forgetting with the light spirit of soldiers both what they themselves had endured, and the anguish of their suffering comrades. The garb of all was in the most miserable and tattered condition, showing how soon the gaudy uniform of the soldier is tarnished in the tug of actual war. Falstaff's wretched band of followers did not exhibit more diversity in the colour and fashion of their habiliments than did these followers of an imperial prince.

One poor ragged wretch in a darkly stained red jacket, with a wisp of clotted canvas round his head, lay on his back helpless, without arms or legs, and totally blind. A cannon had burst close to him, and inflicted on him those injuries which must render him henceforward dependent on the bounty and kindness of others. I was informed that his mental sufferings from seeing himself reduced to such a miserable condition were so severe that they had partially affected his mind, and some fears were entertained that he might never recover the use of his faculties. His, in fact, was one of those cases in which mental eclipse would almost be the greatest of mercies. It was sad to see the poor fellow moving the stumps of his arms to and fro like fishes' fins, as they appeared to me; while from time to time some rough comrade tended him gently, and fed him like an infant.

These men, the followers of an emperor, were the intended regenerators of a barbarous state, the agents of the bright spirit of civilization; and what was their state now as they lay there, prostrate in filth, overcome by sorrow, suffering from wounds, and overrun with vermin? They were all swathed in the foul old clothes they had begged by the way, or tricked out in faded remnants of old uniforms, some of them spotted with blood, and others, that had perhaps belonged to officers, covered with rusty patches of gold lace. It is always a sad sight to see misery like this that one cannot relieve, and we were glad when our eyes no longer rested on such illustrations of the pomp and circumstance of glorious war. We came across them afterwards at Havre, enclosed in a sort of sheep-pen at a railway station. The mob were jeering at them through the railings, and the gentle passed them with a sigh.

After a pleasant passage, we glided quickly into the port of Havre, and landed amidst a jargon of bad English and worse French, the British Cockney preferring to explain all manner of difficulties in a foreign tongue, however imperfectly understood, while the cocked-hatted individual whom he addressed manfully persisted in his endeavours to make everything intelligible in his own peculiar mode of speaking the English language. Here at Le Havre, all good little boys and girls should remember, Bernardin de St. Pierre, the author of "Paul and Virginia" was born; also Casimir

Delavigne. Here, too, Henry the Seventh embarked *en route* for Bosworth Field; and close by is Honfleur, where most of the new-laid eggs that one gets in London come from. Two thousand dozen are despatched per week to England.

Delightful old Rouen, city of a hundred memories, sitting by the winding waters of the Seine, which glide like memories away! Where can we go now-a-days, in this blessed nineteenth century, to see a city so complete an embodiment of the past? Perhaps Pompeii; certainly not the boulevards, the gas-lit streets, and the flaming shops of the generality of French towns. However, there before us is the glorious old cathedral, the handiwork of our Norman ancestors, defying shocks, storms, and time. The Gothic façade, the impression produced by which is so imposing, is a miracle of profuse lace-work petrified; and the dark towers and pinnacles, which rise high over all, are so richly ornamented as to resemble filigree work.

We lift a heavy curtain, and facing us as we enter, motionless, on a high stool placed in a corner, sits an awful creature, completely draped in a costume of coarse black serge, with bent head deeply veiled. It seems some living thing from a few low moans which issue occasionally from underneath the drapery, but otherwise is without form, though it can scarcely be called void. A pale skeleton hand nevertheless now and then slowly turns from one side to another a tin box full of copper coins. Throughout the live-long days, year after year, sits this dismal-looking being, concealing, it may be, beneath that dark veil and hood, some mystery which excites a painfully intense curiosity as one stands in its presence amongst the tombs and gloom of the old cathedral.

The grand Gothic arches are lofty and beautifully proportioned, meeting above and lessening away into perspective, like the great avenue of some old forest of an earlier world, with its stems and foliage now turned into everlasting stone. The large rose-windows let in from the day without floods of rich and mellow lights, colouring the dim, heavy air with a splendid diversity of hue. The chaunt of gaudily-robed priests rises upward with the pomp and incense of High Mass, and a dark crowd kneels on the cold stones which cover the bones of ancient chivalry. No language can describe the elevation of feeling which one experiences as he treads these solemn aisles where generations of worshippers have in succession raised their thoughts to Heaven. As the organ peals forth its solemn notes we feel inspired by the spirit of devotion, and are sensible of that diviner principle within us which carries the thoughts of man beyond the bounds of time and space. We have heard organs innumerable, but never have we listened to one which produced such an effect as that of which we were sensible on the occasion in question. A perfect storm of passion seemed to be swept from the great pipes, and when that was succeeded by the soft strains of the *voix céleste*, one felt as if he were yielding to the gentle influence of some radiant presence, not of this, but of a better world. When men can produce such music, we may naturally ask if the spirits of the departed are near, quickening the soul of the unconscious musician with a spark of the music-spirit of a higher world? This may be considered by many as wild talk; but there are still some human beings who, at least once in their lives, have felt a strain of melody fall with entrancing power upon their hearts, inspiring diviner thoughts than they had ever known before, and so subliming the feelings, that for a time they felt a consciousness of their heavenly origin. He who has never experienced an enthusiasm like this can have no soul for music, but must be entirely of the earth, earthy—"only a clod."

Near the high altar the lion-heart of Richard I. of England was buried. It is now in a very shrunken state, enclosed in a casket, and kept in the museum. It was left as a legacy to Rouen, for which favour no doubt the good inhabitants have been very grateful up to the present hour. His body is in the undisturbed possession of the population of Fontevrault.

Notwithstanding all the modern improvements which have swept away most of ancient Rouen, there still remain some wonderful old quarters, where the crazy wooden houses of centuries back nod towards each other, in a general state of paralysis, across the dark and narrow streets. How they manage to stand at all, leaning upon one another for support, is a mystery; and why they don't sit down bodily upon their occupants is a subject of painful speculation to those good people. It is most interesting to wander in the nooks and corners of this solemn old city; and if the visitor loses his way in the narrow old streets, he may come unexpectedly upon some venerable remnant of antiquity. In many parts every turn reveals some splendid relic of bygone days, of an age of cross-bows, of processions headed by men-at-arms bearing naming braziers through the dark streets, of gallant companies of splendid dames, and flaunting cavaliers in slashed doublets, trunk hose, and inconveniently long swords, all flashing and clanking in the glare as they pass; of an age of night broils, when the clash of arms was heard beneath the dark tower, grated window, and overhanging eaves. Within that ancient palace, ploughed and seamed from gabled roof to the carved monsters on the balustrades beneath, with one rich mass of florid Gothic fretwork, armorial bearings, and quaint gargoyles, we might see the cruel Cardinal of Winchester pacing to and fro in the oak-panelled hall, fretting that the preparations in the square outside, for the burning of Jeanne d'Arc, were proceeding so slowly as to make him late for dinner.

Of course we are not going to describe Rouen and its wonderful architectural remains, nor conjure up visions of mailed Norman chiefs, nursed in war, whose unscrupulous will and iron hearts, backed by the moral weight of great warrior prelates, enforced submission upon all races between Normandy and the far East, from their stern old capital at Rouen. Tempting as is the subject, we have no intention of entering upon any disquisition regarding the vigorous race who founded the city, or of describing the antiquarian relics of which it possesses so rich a store.

It is pleasant to ascend the Mont St. Catherine, and look down upon the fine old town, with its broken walls and ramparts, which have witnessed the gallant struggles of the stout hearts of earlier days, which opposed the onset of Henry V. of England and Henry of Navarre, now overgrown with hoar moss or buried in labyrinths of modern streets, with scarce a thought bestowed upon the past of those mighty chiefs who in old times assailed or defended them—men who, by their deeds, laid the foundations of modern history. It is pleasant to see and feel the solemn air of repose or gentle majesty which hangs over the more silent streets where still stand those time-honoured buildings, the fortresses, palaces, and convents, with piles of toppling planks and wooden turrets, witnesses of ancient story and actors in its varied scenes. There, from the midst of the venerable city, spire up to the level of the wood-crowned heights surrounding Rouen, the fretted pinnacles of the cathedral towers, and beneath them the gables of Gothic houses pierce the air, while afar off the silver windings of the Seine, studded with green islets, lose themselves in the mist which hangs in the distance, seaward.

In the city below died the simple-minded, heroic, and betrayed Maid of Orleans. There, forsaken by his own sons, and his menials even, in agony and neglect, William, the Conqueror of England, and of our Saxon Harold, departed this life. There died also the great Clarendon; and there Corneille and Boieldieu were born.

It is pleasant to look at all this from afar, but very unpleasant to be in the midst thereof; for it is a remarkable fact, alike observable in Cologne as in Rouen, that the more historical the city, the more horrible the smells. Coleridge counted in the former city a certain and distinct number of odours vile; we wonder to what numerals his inquiring nose would have extended itself at Rouen. The prevailing type of flavour in the latter city seems to be a compound of extra-sour vinegar, stale slop pails, and burnt india-rubber. It is also unpleasant to be ferried over a rapid river in a thing like a worn-out gondola, with several holes in the direction of the keel, the portentous effects of which the strenuous baling powers of two men with a sardine box and a coffee cup could scarcely allay. It was, however, observed of us before we embarked, by a funny friend who accompanied us, and whose miserable puns often made us melancholy, that if we trusted ourselves to such a craft we should be *in Seine.*

No one in these parts, excepting idiots or princes, being in the habit of travelling in a first-class carriage, we started in a second (we mean no pun) *en route* for Le Mans, in the fresh and healthy society of some young Norman peasant girls. No abominable chignon disfigured the backs of their neat little heads, for there was no necessity with them to shine with borrowed plumes. Their smooth hair was neatly arranged beneath the small linen cap of snowy white, while a striped kerchief was drawn modestly across the breast. "There is no joy without alloy," however, and certainly the old peasant woman up in the corner, with a bottle of red acid liquor and a stout staff of bread—the real staff of life—guarding-like a halberdier the well-closed windows, did not strike the eye as anything peculiarly attractive, excepting perhaps at times, when, from the red acid which she occasionally imbibed, her face took a sympathetic tone, and being completely encircled by her large frill, produced an effect which a rather extravagant imagination might regard as something like that of the setting sun in a nightcap. The girls were young—*she*, doubtless, at some time or other had been so too; but grey moustaches are not generally associated with any distinct type of beauty in ladies. Notwithstanding the aforesaid head-gear she certainly could not be pronounced *cap*-tivating as our punning friend said and, wonderful to say, she knew it!

Our train passed through Lisieux, where Henry II. was married to Eleanor of Guienne, and where the modern inhabitants are chiefly employed in the manufacture of horse clothing and general flannelry. Near this not very striking town, M. Guizot spends his summer months, and in it, by-the-by, Thomas à Becket passed his banishment in 1169. About four o'clock P.M. our train turned us out high and dry, bag and baggage, on to a lonely wooden platform in the midst of a dreary flat tract of country, compared with which Cambridgeshire is extremely steep and alpine.

"Où sommes-nous donc?" asked we.

"À Mezidon, m'sieu," said an official. "Deux heures d'attente."

We immediately left our luggage with this trusty man, set our watches by the clocks of the *gare*, pulled our hats with determination on to our heads, and walked desperately four miles straight along a dusty high road, then turned round and walked four miles back; by which time the train was ready to start again.

CHAPTER II.

LE MANS.—ANCIENT CITY BY NIGHT.—THE LUXURY OF BATHING.—CATHEDRAL OF ST. JULIEN.—TOURS.—POITIERS.—ANGOULÊME.—BORDEAUX.—EN ROUTE FOR BAYONNE.—A MERCANTILE DEFAULTER.—A LONELY REGION.—HOTEL INTERIOR.—INGENIOUS INVENTION.—TABLE D'HÔTE.

AT midnight Le Mans was reached, amidst a deluge of rain and an insufficiency of street lamps. Gas, we believe, has found its way to Jerusalem, but not to Le Mans; and yet Le Mans is a large and important town, blessed with an enlightened and despotic government.

After settling ourselves, to our extreme inconvenience, in a vehicle like an opera-box drawn side-ways by a horse and bells, we bumped and jingled slowly on through long, dark streets, the houses in which were all so large and gloomy that they looked like prisons, and in which there appeared to be a general flushing of sewers.

Le Mans may or may not be the "trodden ground" our critics complain of, but we are quite sure it was not so when we arrived there, for not a living thing was seen in the great black town save a benighted cat or two and one very ancient rag-picker. A more forsaken and deserted-looking place could not be imagined—no, not even by Daniel the Prophet, with all his experience of "the abomination of desolation," &c.

The grey light of the skies showed us at last a great square opening before us, with a lofty stone building like a war tower rising dark in the midst. We stopped at an inn door in this square, and descended, the opera-box making a vigorous plunge to assist us in the operation. Repeated pulls at a cracked bell, which sounded dismally in some remote depth of the old house, eventually produced the effect desired, for a rattling of chains was heard, and then the heavy door swung slowly on its hinges, sufficiently to admit of the protrusion of a man's head. The head came out as far as the shoulders, and nothing more ghastly could be conceived, as for a few seconds it remained there motionless and isolated against the black background, like the decapitated skull of some malefactor nailed to a gibbet, the face gleaming deadly in the uncertain night-light. The dreary silence of the dark square was broken only by the lonely cry of some distant watchman, pacing the old streets here and there with a dull lamp, which served to deepen still more the darkness beyond, whilst, high, gaunt, and spectral against the dull grey air, loomed the fortress-like building. A gigantic lighted clock was poised on a high tower, the long hands thereof making great leaps of five minutes each along the dial, as if it were dozing, and then suddenly waking and making up for lost time by desperate strides. In fact, to anyone who had recently supped upon pork chops, or to the cheerful mind of the late lamented Mrs. Anne Radcliffe, of raw-head-and-bare-bones memory, this old tower and its clock might have appeared as the Ogre Time, or some huge Cyclopean ghoul of night, watching and gloating, with its burning eye, over the surely passing hours of the thousand slumberers lying for a season sweetly unconscious of the fleeting of life beneath, and counting each heave of breath which as it passes must bring all nearer and nearer to its maw.

The waiter who belonged to the head before mentioned turned out to be a most excellent young man, and, in his assiduous exertions to make himself agreeable to apparently the first British traveller he had ever beheld, danced about like an electrified frog. Indeed, we were grateful enough for this very sprightliness of his, for it acted as a corrective to the depressing effect of the entire establishment, which was pervaded by an air of dull, forlorn gloom. The walls appeared to be constantly in tears. The long cavernous passages and mysterious corridors were made doubly dark by the sulky gleam of a consumptive "short ten." The lofty bedrooms were provided with beds which had too close a resemblance to four-post hearses, and their furniture in general had too much of the faded grandeur of other days. The old wooden staircases creaked audibly before we began to walk upon them, as if some invisible ghost of a dead housemaid were waiting to show us up to bed, and when we ventured upon them we found they were leaning alarmingly on one side. We endeavoured as well as we could to keep in the middle, but they were so unsteady that their movement produced a sensation like that of mild intoxication or incipient sea-sickness. We were not without dread lest, supposing the balustrades showed equal signs of weakness, we might, if we did not hug the wall and coast along it very carefully, be shovelled neck and crop into the abyss below. Can anyone wonder, therefore, that in such a place we were grateful for the sprightliness of our waiter, whose good spirits and lively antics prevented us from indulging in depressing thoughts? Variety of any kind is pleasing. Who has not heard of the gentleman who got into such a depressed condition of mind from attending the debates in the House of Lords and the burlesques at the London theatres, that, with the view of obtaining a little beneficial change, he took occasional walks in Brompton Cemetery, attended executions at the Old Bailey, or paid frequent visits to an anatomical museum? It was the same gentleman who was said always to carry an umbrella with an ivory death's-head as the handle, who had a velvet coat made from a piece of his wife's pall, and who took to singing the songs of Claribel.

Le Mans is a grand old town, stately, but mouldy and only half alive. Throughout there is happily an absence of that white garish Parisian element. No whitewash, gilded railings, or sculptured gewgaws offend the genius of the spot. The solemn old houses and walls stand looking down on the quiet streets as sadly as on that day when the last remnant of the gallant Vendean army under Larochejaquelein, wearied with the toils of long campaigns, was cut to pieces beneath them in the year 1793. The face of the old town seems as sorrowful now as when the shrieks of dying women and children, remorselessly slaughtered before it by the conquering Republicans, died away upon the air, on that day when cannonades of grape and volleys of musketry swept through all the streets, among a helpless crowd of the wretched wives and little ones of the scattered Royalists, of whom ten thousand corpses lay red in that awful sunset.

In the early morning we nearly frightened to death some good citizens by bathing in the river Sarthe, and several crowded to the bank to witness the last gasps of two insane victims to the love of ablution. It was a fine warm day in September, yet the idea to them seemed madness. However, this little adventure brought to light what Diogenes had so long sought for—an honest man. As we were drying ourselves on the river bank, beneath the shadows of the old cathedral on the height above, a passer-by in course of conversation observed,—

"*Pour moi, messieurs*, I detest water—never touch it—*ni chaude, ni froide.*"

Now we like this blunt truthfulness, so much better than the big talk of some people respecting their tubs and baths, who yet never go near them. We remember, upon one occasion, in a country house there was a gentleman who was always talking about the luxury of "tubbing," and whose constant refrain was, "What a brute a man must be who doesn't tub," &c. Being the occupant of the adjoining room to us, we happened, quite by accident, one fine morning, upon hearing a tremendous splashing and dashing, to look through the key-hole, and discovered, much to our astonishment, our friend standing up, half dressed, in knickerbockers, shirt, and diamond pin, squeezing a sponge into a tin bath, and shouting in a very loud whisper (which would have made his fortune in an "aside" on the stage), as if overpowered with the freshness of the water, "Oh! how delightful! By Jove, how cold! Ahi! phew! a—h! oh!"

The cathedral of St. Julien is a grand, imposing Gothic structure, grey with the hoar of age. Its lofty towers, which are so richly ornamented that they appear as if covered with fretwork, hang at a great elevation above the city, crowning a height. In it we found the monument of Berengaria of Sicily, Queen of Richard I. of England, and the tomb of Charles of Anjou.

Le Mans has the honour of having given birth to Henry II., the first Plantagenet king of England; and we suppose we ought here to mention, what every one on earth must know, that his father Geoffroi always wore in his cap a sprig of genêt, or broom, which grows luxuriantly throughout Maine and Anjou, and hence the name of a race of kings—Plante-a-genêt.

From Le Mans we took the railway to Tours. Upon nearing that city we passed an old red château, where Louis XI. shut himself up, dreading, like Oliver Cromwell and many great criminals, daily assassination. Gates within gates, castle within castle, like a remarkably strong Chinese ball-puzzle; such is the interior. On a plain near Tours—an old story—Charles Martel beat the Saracens in 731. No one writes on Tours who does not say, "If the Saracens had beaten Charles Martel, we should all be keeping harems, smoking tchibouques, and praying on bits of square carpets, or, whenever we had a moment or two to spare, on turnpike roads," &c.

After we had passed Tours the country was flat, ugly, and very uninteresting. Poitiers, which we reached in due course, is a picturesque, battlemented old town, built on the tops of precipices, the sides of hills, rocks, and ravines, with green slopes, gardens, and river. We say nothing about the Black Prince, Lord Chandos, and King John, at the battle of Poitiers. We wonder, indeed, if they were ever there; for was there not a man who once wrote a book to prove that there had been no such person as Napoleon?

After passing Angoulême, at which we stopped for a short interval, it became too dark to see or read, and we tried to sleep; but soon discovered what a quantity of hitherto unknown and extraordinary bumps and sharp angles the human form possesses. In spite, however, of our discomforts, the train rattled on, and we arrived at Bordeaux. After a good night's rest, the disagreeable effects of our journey disappeared; and getting up fresh and active in the morning, we set out to explore the city. But what did we see? Docks, *et præterea nihil.*

As we were taking our seats in the train for Bayonne, we perceived in the next carriage to us, guarded by three gendarmes, a pale, middle-aged man of gentle exterior, at whom several persons at the carriage window were hurling execrations. Being unfortunate in the management of his affairs, he had attempted to maintain his position by means which brought him within the clutch of the law, and the consequence was loss and ruin, not only to himself, but also to many who had placed entire confidence in his integrity. Now, doubtless, he regretted his folly, and formed many good intentions as to the future; but, alas, several years must pass over before he can put them into practice, and when he emerges once more into life, the world will laugh to scorn the fine sentiments of a man out of jail, and, securely mailed in the panoply of their own good luck,—we beg its pardon, high morality,—politely refer him to an observation of Seneca's:—"Quid est turpius quam senex vivere incipiens?" [1]

However, every proverb has its reverse, "Ogni medaglia ha il suo reverso;" and against Seneca we can pit Mr. Charles Reade, who thinks it "never too late to mend."

We were roused from our reverie by a voice exclaiming, "En voiture, messieurs!" and at the same time the whistle screamed, the bell rang, and that great leveller, the railway train, glided off. In a few minutes the spires and masts of Bordeaux had passed away, and with them every vestige of the bustle and clang of busy life. How strange it seemed that in so short a time we should have dashed into the midst of lonely regions where the tracks of civilization seemed all but lost! Onwards we scoured, over the desolate Landes, over brown trackless moor, and through the gloom of forests. The leaden heavens seemed stagnant and dead, and indeed a ray of sunlight or gleam of warmth in such a scene would seem but a mockery to the heart. On, through desert places where the wild bird and solitary wood-cutter alone quicken the deadness of the silent wastes which spread away in dark expanse to the horizon. Far and wide no life is seen, and no sign thereof, save an occasional group of wretched hovels buried in the recesses of the black woods, which are perceived only for a moment through a storm-torn gap as we fly along and then are gone, leaving the wilderness again in all its dead stillness under the fading light of the dreary skies.

The lights of Bayonne at length gladly broke upon us as the evening darkened, and in a short time we were rattling with horse and bells through the heavy stone gates, and over the moats and drawbridges of the city walls. The old narrow streets, with their tall houses covered with balconies, lattices, and coloured blinds, were a foretaste of those to be seen in Spain. The rows of lighted shops, beneath heavy low arcades built of hewn stone, and supported by stout pillars, brown with age, were all crowded with busy passengers, garbed with sash, velvet breech, and bonnet. The bright cafés—filled with loungers, small politicians, and trim waiters, with their hair mowed to the roots—were shedding on the roadway floods of yellow light.

On we rattled, over roads not paved yesterday, if ever paved at all, amidst bumping and jingling, forced to listen from time to time to periodic fits of shocking language addressed to the smoking horses, gay in coloured trappings, and trotting us merrily along. Now we dived into a narrow alley, black as pitch darkness could make it. Then we twisted out of it so sharply, round a corner, that, had our hair not been carefully oiled, it would have stood on end, and emerged into a wide street full of gas lamps, illuminated windows, and rows of bright green little trees, trimmed so artificially that they had as little resemblance to their natural growing congeners as those in a child's Noah's ark. It was pleasant, after our dreary day's journey, to find ourselves thus hurrying, in the brilliant flare of the night lamps, through a most picturesque old town, over bridges from which we could see in the rapid waters below the twinkling reflection of a hundred lights, along streets in which we passed companies of soldiers marching to the music of drums and bugles, and through busy quays all alive with bustle and loaded with merchandise. In fact,

"The city gates were opened; the market, all alive

With buyers and with sellers, was humming like a hive;

Blithely on brass and timber the craftsman's stroke was ringing;

And blithely o'er her panniers the peasant girl was singing."

And "blithely" we eventually entered the Hotel * * *, and sat down to a remarkably good dinner of fresh sardines, wild boar, *paté de foie de canard*, and a dish of *beccaficoes*. "Our bore," the inevitable Cockney across the table, fired off a sickly joke at the expense of those little birds, to the effect that, if we had never yet eaten *beccaficoes*, we ought-to-learn (*ortolan*). Now really! Oh! who can minister to the "mind diseased" that produces such monstrosities?

The hotel was a great square house, with a wonderful collection of keys on a board by the entrance door, as if they had been fired there like grape-shot out of a gun. The passages and staircases were liberally supplied by day with sand and saliva, and by night with cockroaches of remarkable size. Hanging on the walls of the *salle-à-manger* were advertisements of bull-fights to come off in various towns of Spain, and also others of various hotels in different countries. There was one of a boarding-house in Weymouth Street, Portland Place, London, with a picture of the same. Now we do not wish to set up as art-critics, but merely state that we have once or twice in the course of our lives had occasion to find ourselves in that salubrious district, but don't remember noticing any detached house or Italian villa in a park, with palm trees waving over it, and a plantain in full growth. There was another picture of a hotel in Granada, with the Moors walking about the streets and conversing with the waiters at the door, as if Abderrhaman was still residing in Spain.

In the courtyard of our inn a fountain was playing, and a vine formed a large shady arbour for smokers and idlers beneath. There was not much to complain of, and notwithstanding the general smell of garlic, and an odour resembling that of steamboat cabins, with which the bedrooms were perfumed, we slept most comfortably for a short time with calm consciences and clean sheets, gratefully manufacturing a proverb for the occasion, to the effect that fine feathers make fine beds, to say nothing of good housemaids. We even glided into dreams, in which we held conversations with individuals of every possible complexion, dressed in scarlet Scotch bonnets, velveteen jackets, broken out into a nettle-rash of metal buttons, red sashes, breeches, and hose, in Basque, Spanish, French, English, and all sorts of patois, all at once, and with incredible ease, coherence, and velocity. We say we slept most comfortably for a short time, and one must have been very deaf, or stolid, or philosophical,—in a word, insensible to all sorts of disturbance,—to have slept comfortably after 2 A.M. in such a place. For diligence after diligence coming from somewhere or other, and going in the same direction, rolled by every quarter of an hour immediately underneath our windows, accompanied with loud shouts, cracking of whips, and jangling of bells.

Between the quarters of the hours a gentleman and his wife enlightened the entire hotel with a domestic wrangle in one of the rooms in our neighbourhood, and at 5 A.M. some person or persons overhead, probably experimentalising with a cold tub for the first time in their lives, apparently found it impossible to restrain themselves from giving vent to the natural exhilaration produced by the bath in what seemed, by the trampling they made, to be an Indian war-dance. Added to this, there was a clock in our apartment which struck six when it should have struck four, and eight when it should have struck six, thereby becoming a source of much anxiety to the half-dormant mind, torturing it with vague speculations when it should have been at rest.

The bedroom bell was ingenious enough, going off like an alarum when a knob of wood fixed in the wall was touched; and the invention would be still more valuable if it would at the same time induce any servants to answer it. As it was, the only chance, after prodding it for a good quarter of an hour without any other result than a sore thumb and a great deal of noise, was to seat oneself in an arm-chair before it with the latest newspaper, or some interesting book, and, the elbow firmly pressed against the knob, so to remain, if needs be, for the whole afternoon until some one below was sick of the rattle, and condescended to come and inquire the cause of the summons.

A *table-d'hôte* breakfast in places like Bayonne is very trying to a delicate stomach, especially when an opposite lady is in the habit of wearing a false nose, and when the gentlemen wear diamond rings and very dirty wristbands. Individuals of excited imaginations may possibly regale themselves with *potage à paté d'Italie*, but to minds of ordinary level it appears but as some mystic and not very inviting fluid with things like boiled gentles in it. *Rognons sautés en champagne* is a dish also considered by the sanguine as something quite unique, whereas a philosopher (at all events at so early a meal as breakfast) is apt to connect that condiment in a general way with old hats and hot water.

FOOTNOTE:

[1] What is more miserable than to see an old man just entering on the practice of virtue?

CHAPTER III.

THE CITADEL.—BIARRITZ.—HOW THE VISITORS KILL TIME.—EN ROUTE FOR SPAIN.—ST. JEAN DE LUZ.—HENDAYE.—THE BIDASSOA CROSSED.—WINTER IN SPAIN.—IRUN.—CUSTOM-HOUSE OFFICIALS.—ST. SEBASTIAN.—THE ALAMEDA PROMENADE.—THE PLAIN OF VITTORIA.

WHEN after breakfast we looked out of our window, we perceived on the opposite side of the way a grim old castle, with little grated windows sunk deep into its walls, like the eyes in a consumptive face. And well, indeed, should that old building hide its eyes from all creation, for did not its walls give shelter to the guilty trio who planned within them the devilish scheme of the massacre of St. Bartholomew,—the Duke of Alva, Catherine de' Medici, and her miserable offspring, Charles IX.?

A walk about Bayonne brings to notice of course a great amount of fortification, especially the citadel of Vauban, where Marshal Soult and the Duke of Wellington fought very hard and sacrificed a great number of the soldiers of their respective countries. Proceeding in another direction outside the town, the tourist will come to a cemetery where lie forgotten, mouldering in the dust of a foreign land, the remains of the officers of the British guards who fell during the fruitless siege of Bayonne. Down in a dim dell, amongst old trees whispering a requiem in the breeze of falling night, we stood over those solitary graves, near which there was no sign of life, and where the brambles of the wilderness did their utmost to impede the tributary footsteps of the two English pilgrims to this forgotten shrine of their brave countrymen, on which the last beams of sunset threw what seemed in imagination a bloody light.

On a fine southern morning, we climbed on to the top of a crazy diligence, swinging in a very top-heavy and uncomfortable manner over some very high wheels. The vehicle swayed to and fro in such a way that the last carriage of an express train on the narrow gauge would appear immovable compared with it. The *banquette*, with its hood, in which we were travelling for pleasure, seemed quite overburdened with politeness, and bowed in the most humble manner to everybody and everything it met. We were now on our way to Biarritz, a place we reached after an hour's drive in which there is nothing very remarkable to attract the traveller's attention.

Biarritz is a town situated on the shores of the Bay of Biscay, and consists chiefly of hotels and boarding-houses built on rocks. It is peopled generally by emperors, waiters, hawkers of spurious Spanish goods, and very idle ladies and gentlemen. Creatures like mermaids, with their extremities encased in mackintosh, are seen nearly all day long sporting about in the waters which break upon the yellow sand, and dancing quadrilles in the sea with very odd-looking fish of the male gender, also swathed in curious garments, which cause them at a little distance to resemble very badly rolled-up umbrellas, or an imperfect class of sausages. Barring the bathing, the amusements of Biarritz, or Biarits, as some of the natives write it, are very dear and rather silly. People revolve nightly on their own axes to the solemn strains of a horn band in a large casino, with expressions of countenance as serious and business-like as if they were undergoing a course of rotatory exercise recommended by their medical advisers as a stimulant after the chills of the bath; while the day is consumed, one hardly knows how, except it be in flirting, aquatics, scandal, abuse of one's neighbours, or in buying from gaudy coffee-coloured Spaniards trumpery which, under no conceivable circumstances, could the most ingenious mind ever turn to any account. There is certainly grand food for the eye whichever way it may turn, "whene'er we take our walks abroad," for the long jagged line of the Spanish mountains is seen, now clear, dark, and sharp, now wild and storm-wrapped, rising loftily from the far blue main; and there is always playing on one's cheek, or with the flowing tress of many a pretty damsel, the pure strengthening air of the Bay of Biscay, sweeping with untainted breath from across the dark, wild waves of the rolling Atlantic. From the summits of the various sea-worn rocks and pinnacles which jut out from the land may be seen beautiful views of the white amphitheatre of Biarritz, formed by clusters of villas, casinos, and bathing pavilions along the curving shore, or piled on gentle hills, rising one above the other in picturesque confusion, with their sunny walls shaded here and there by green shrubberies, or gay with flaunting banners waving over shining terrace and grassy slope, the stately Villa Eugénie of the Empress commanding the whole. In front the restless waves are ever rolling in on the yellow sands, in their ceaseless chase from the Bay of Biscay, spread out so broad, blue, and beautiful; while to the south the distant skies seem walled up by that grand dark chain of the Spanish mountains, towering through clouds and tempests in wild and lofty grandeur, or melting away on the far horizon into the heat of the golden day and the spume of the tossing sea.

The people at Biarritz seem to be in a chronic state of masquerade. In some the disease takes a severe and malignant form, in others simply that of a mild and harmless lunacy. Very fierce and dirty individuals prowl about the streets, in what is popularly supposed to be the Spanish costume, namely, shabby velveteen inexpressibles, jackets covered with a perfect eruption of buttons and bobbins, and the calves of their legs swathed in linen bandages, as if they were in a general state of poultice. These individuals have dreadful long Spanish knives to sell, knives which, when any Englishman is so infatuated as to decline buying Birmingham cutlery at Biarritz, they grasp in a very portentous manner, opening and shutting them with an air of determination which is most alarming to the weak and nervous.

"Who comes in foreign trashery

Of tinkling chain and spur,

A walking haberdashery

Of feathers, lace, and fur?"

Who indeed? the poet might well ask on the afternoon parade at Biarritz; and it is not at all certain that the people know themselves. There are gentlemen in short white jackets made of blanket, lemon-coloured tights, and Napoleon boots, or in knickerbockers and top-boots, Scotch plaids, and very tall hats, with brims so narrow as to be rather problematical. The British traveller is, of course, to be seen there, as everywhere else, with a beard in that state which one does not know whether to attribute to neglect or intention.

The ladies simply *dress at* one another, and the extravagance of their costumes can only be conceived by minds of the calibre of Gilray, or by such as can picture to themselves Paris fashion gone mad. We saw one lady in short skirts and Hessian boots, with little bells for tassels. The dress itself was so stiff with embroidery and needlework that it would have made a capital diving-bell; and the jacket was so profusely embroidered with lace that it seemed made of solid gold. Nearly every lady finds it necessary, for some at present inscrutable reason,—which, however, like other mysteries will some day be made known,—to walk about with a slender white wand with a nail at the end. What are these sticks? Are they fetishes, or are they connected with any form of superstition. Why are they adorned with nails? And for what reason are they carried like toothpicks between the finger and thumb of a tight kid-gloved hand? We should also like to ask why do young English ladies at foreign *tables d'hôte* always appear as if somebody was perpetually on the point of whispering something improper to them? Their frightened air, indeed, as one out of common politeness prepares to address them with some commonplace remark, is so infectious that it is a wonder one does not fall plump into a perfect mire of mistakes and *gaucheries*, a miserable martyr to the cause of amiability.

It certainly is a marvel how people manage to thrive on the fare provided at these entertainments,—ghostly entertainments, we may call them,—for there, as surely as the clock tolls forth the hour, appears the spectre "cock and salad," which, with the perversity of fate, ever haunts the path of the European tourist, to scare and depress his appetite. The old philosopher, in observing

"Ὁ ἀνθρωπος εὐεργετος πεφυκως," [2]

must have had some prophetic revelation of the after-times of modern civilization, and particularly of Biarritz *tables d'hôte*; for if man was not naturally a benevolent creature how could he endure with equanimity day after day the same plateful of luke-warm water—*potage à l'eau chaude*, it ought to be called—apparently stirred up with a tallow candle to give it a flavour; the same recurring square phids of old dry rug (rosbif) of which the soup was made; the same *perdreaux aux choux*, which sound so magnificent in theory, but when reduced to sad reality consist mainly of *choux* and the bones of some small specimens of the feathered tribe? Then the *filets de bœuf*—can they be made of old door-mats?—what labour must one undergo before he can persuade the "too solid flesh to melt!"

At these gastronomic revels we are sure to meet an English paterfamilias, with mamma and daughters. When we say English, we do not mean moderately English, but downright and awfully British—British in the dogged look of plethoric, stupid self-complacency and general superiority over everybody and everything not British—British in that moneyed bovine state of mind which distinguishes the inferior specimens of the *nouveau riche* fresh from Albion. The mamma and daughters, too, are British to a degree, as they sit enveloped in a dull atmosphere of Clapham gentility, striving to their utmost to appear easy and graceful "at meals and in company." But in spite of these laudable endeavours, it is a difficult point to decide which is preferable to witness—the alarming efforts of people endeavouring to eat and drink elegantly, holding their knives and forks like pens, and a wine-glass between a finger and thumb, with the rest of the fingers outstretched to their fullest tension, ending in the little finger pointing away in far perspective; or honestly at once scratching themselves with a spoon, lapping up gravy with a knife at the fearful risk of widening their mouths to the extent of the aperture of a letter-box, and when thirsty taking a hearty draught of water from the finger-basins. As for the *juste milieu* people talk about, that at most *tables d'hôte* seems quite Utopian and might form an innocent branch of study for the Reform League.

Bathing goes on during the whole morning and afternoon, and the method is in this wise. We walk down across the sands from the bathing cabinets, a distance of a hundred and fifty yards, barefooted, like some ancient friar going on a pilgrimage. We are wrapt in the white flowing folds of a long garment resembling a Knight Templar's cloak, and are attended in state by two men rolled up in oil-cloth. When we have arrived at the brink of the sea, our attendants venture in with us to a depth perhaps of twelve inches, and we are recommended by them to put a little water into the hollow of the hand and pour it carefully on to the top of the head. This ordeal being safely accomplished, we commence a polite little dance hand-in-hand with one of the bathing men in the presence of the crowd—it may be the whole town—on the beach. After jumping up a few times as high as possible, in order to avoid every wave as it approaches, the two bathing attendants inquire after Monsieur's health, and how he carries himself—*comment se porte-il?*—and finally they lead us back by the tips of our fingers, and on the points of their toes, across the sandy plain, still in full view of the assembled populace, to the row of sentry boxes or cabinets on the grand parade, where we pass in a very depressed condition through the centre of a large concourse of splendidly attired ladies and gentlemen. If we are in luck, perhaps an old lady or two may smile blandly at us as we pass, as if to congratulate us on our escape from the perils we have encountered. If we wish to keep in the highest *mode*, a slight walking-stick or cane is considered an elegant and useful accompaniment to the bath.

Young ladies are conducted singly into the water in the same manner by the men in mackintosh, and upon these occasions they seem to disport themselves in the most playful manner. They of course do not neglect this opportunity of adorning themselves with the most singular costumes, and look in their tunics, trousers, and straw hats very androgynous. They never wet their heads, and on their return deposit their feet immediately in very hot water, to draw the blood from the brain. We preferred, however, to bathe in our own native style, and found it very pleasant to walk into the sea at the Port Vieux, and swim out, far away from bathers and bathees, until we could disport in the open sea. We swam past the two opposite capes which form the entrance to the little bay, where the buoyant water supports us as a sofa; and from the bosom of the deep, on which we reclined, we enjoyed the splendid panorama of the distant Pyrenees which our own unaided efforts had procured us. It is pleasant to stand on any of the island rocks of Biarritz and hear the great waves below dash amidst the caverns they have hewn out, sounding like far artillery. It is amusing, when one is not in a critical mood, to meet a funny Briton now and then at the *table d'hôte*, who tells you little innocent lies to the effect that his uncle, being evangelical, had four sons named Matthew, Mark, Luke, and John, and when a fifth was born, called him "The Acts of the Apostles." But the most pleasant thing of all is to find one's back turned, after a sojourn of four days, upon this stupid little town, where there is so much frivolity and, curious as it may seem, no less dulness.

Eh bien, nous voici enfin well started for Spain! We reflected we should arrive at Burgos at twelve at night. However (as a Spanish railway accident is an awful affair), better late than never. The hotels would, no doubt, all be closed, and we should find ourselves in rather an awkward position. We neither speak nor understand a word of Spanish, but the people at Burgos are much in the same predicament, as they have a patois or dialect of their own. Most of the silver money of the country is bad, and the keepers of hotels or *fondas* in Spain, are as *fond as* (the author of this bright idea was our funny friend) innkeepers in England of practising a little harmless extortion upon travellers,—in fact, *fonder*.

We passed St. Jean de Luz, a queer tumble-down old town on the borders of the sea, in whose cathedral the Grand Monarque was married to Maria Theresa, daughter of Philip IV. of Spain, and in the great red house in the square the happy couple lived for a fortnight or so in nuptial beatitude. Some way off rises the mountain of Bayonnetta, down whose slopes a spirited band of peasants once charged their enemies with poles, to the ends of which they had lashed their long-bladed knives. Some find in this fact the origin of the bayonet. The town is inhabited by whale-fishers, a few soldiers, and some centipedes.

When we arrived, the loungers at the station were still talking over the recent accident which had well nigh upset all the calculations that Napoleon III. has made as to his dynasty. The sea is generally very rough at the entrance to the little harbour; and on the occasion in question, as the Empress was landing in a small boat from her steamer, the boat was upset close to land. The Empress and Prince both struck out, the one shouting as much as was consistent with a mouthful of water, "Save my son!" the other, "Save my mother!" This was as it should be. Eugénie and the heir to the imperial throne were saved, but the poor pilot was drowned.

We shortly reached Hendaye, the last French town, and the Bidassoa, which here divides the two countries, was crossed. There are some low swampy lands visible at low water between the sea and the bridge over the river, and no one but amphibious creatures would, one would imagine, venture upon them. In 1813, the Duke of Wellington, however, persuaded his army to wade through them; thereby succeeding in both astonishing Marshal Soult and taking his position.

We next arrived at Irun, the first Spanish town, in a storm of sleet and rain, and in a hurricane of wind. In fact, it had rained, and blown great guns and small arms, almost incessantly for the last four days at Bayonne and Biarritz, and the farther south we got the worse got the weather. People for some inscrutable reason go to Spain for the winter. They had surely better remain in the mild and even climate of Ventnor or Torquay; for if the sample of autumn we were favoured with was supposed to be genial, the Fates and common sense defend us against experimentalising with our miserable bodies upon the Spanish winter! To winter amidst the damps, or rather wets (for damp is a mild expression indeed), the violent winds and the shelterless plains of the north of Spain would, we fancy, be sufficient to send a Laplander into a consumption. What effect it would produce upon a delicate English female, we cannot attempt to decide upon our own authority. We doubt not, however, that Seville, Valencia, Granada, or even Barcelona, with their sunny skies and favourable position, may be more favourable to the invalid, and melt the icy fingers of winter ere they can reach him; though, alas! the frost of death will strike down its victims even under warm and radiant skies. True, it seems at times as if death might be touched with a temporary remorse, and be persuaded to defer the fatal blow; but what matter a few moments longer in a dreary world? Of what value is another year amidst a sea of troubles—an ocean of toils and cares? Whether our life be a dream of sorrow or of bliss, it must shortly end. If the former, why should we care to prolong it? If the latter, it is like the one joyous life-hour of the butterfly,—'tis gone at our sunset, when the poor heart has beaten itself out. The blushing flowers of summer, even as we bend over them, fade, wither, and die; and the music of a woman's whisper faints away even as it is uttered. All that is mortal, all that is lovely, must pass away into darkness, and the objects of our fondest affections must disappear in the shifting sands of Time!

At Irun the *aduaneros*, who are all mustachios and impertinence, are supposed to be very exacting, and one is warned not to look cross or anxious as one's portmanteaux are plumbed, and rummaged, and mauled by the fingers of gentlemen who seem to think that smoking and eating garlic are nearer to godliness than cleanliness. So, taking advantage of this advice, we immediately on our arrival called up a ready-made and vacant smile, and assumed such an air of nonchalance, that the *aduaneros* must have thought we were stupidly regardless of our personal property. One sharp-eyed little official, however, not quite understanding how any sane man could travel about Europe with a washing apparatus, seized greedily upon our friend's india-rubber bath with a little growl of ferocity. This convenient article, as all know, is fluted round the edges; and the little man consequently came to the conclusion that the fluted divisions must constitute some kind of infernal machine, provided with a certain number of barrels, the explosion of which would blow up the Queen of Spain and her Ministry; and that we, of course, were a couple of daring revolutionists. It was with some difficulty that we succeeded in convincing the important official that he was in error, and then we were allowed to proceed.

The rain still descended in cataracts, the wind blew with unrestrained violence, and everything looked damp, dirty, and dull, as we once more entered the railway carriage. Here we rashly fired off a sentence of Spanish in the reckless manner of one who fires off his gun when "Woodcock" is suddenly shouted in a plantation, viz., shutting the eyes, firing in the air, and trusting to Providence.

"*No se cambia coches Burgos?*" gasped we.

"No, señor," answered the guard.

We restrained all further desire for conversation with that functionary, as vain, weak, and unprofitable, for it is said, "Set a beggar on horseback, and he will ride to"—a gentleman not usually mentioned in polite society. But for our part, we make it a golden rule, when we wish to air our French or Italian, never to address persons of a stern aspect, never to make linguistic experiments upon hard-looking men. It is better to single out an individual with a mild and rather fatuous countenance for the purpose in question. We avoid individuals of imposing presence, and seek out humble little men who slink into corners, and, if possible, people of delicate constitution. A quiet young man in spectacles, for instance, who is going to Mentone for health, and who has a box by his side labelled, "*Fragile—Huile de foie de morue*," is a good subject; in fact, any one who is too feeble to be astonished at anything.

As we continued our journey into Spain, the lower spurs of the Pyrenees rose darkly over the sea, and waved away in lofty undulations of vale and mountain, with their slopes up to their summits clothed in green woods, or dotted here and there with pretty Swiss-looking cottages, while through the drifting scud a stray sunbeam occasionally found its way, and ever and anon fell in a flash of glory athwart the golden tints of the autumnal woods.

At length a high citadel and some turret-crested hills came into view, looking down upon a clustering group of grotesque old houses, fishermen's huts and vessels, the masts and sails of merchant craft, while whitewashed Basque cottages were seen in all directions peeping out from thick foliage, and appearing very bright and clean. This was San Sebastian. Here the upper ten thousand of Madrid resort for bathing in the summer season, when the shores of the little bay are turned into a perfect camp of tents, pavilions, and bathing-machines.

The Alameda promenade is crowded on afternoons with hundreds of people in quaint Basque costumes. The bull-ring and the theatre are also favourite resorts of the inhabitants and visitors.

The fair amount of beauty met with amongst the females of this fine semi-barbarous Celtic race occasionally tempts the passing traveller to remain a day or two in this curious and pleasant old town.

All seems so peaceful now in and around San Sebastian, the sleepy quiet of which is broken only by the roar of distant waves, that it is difficult to conjure up the scenes of carnage which, after the defeat of the French garrison by the English, took place here—the rush of hissing shot, the crash of falling houses, and the shrieks of women and children dying midst flames and smoke! Who can imagine the condition of a town given up to drunken soldiers, maddened with lust, success, and wine? England has glorious annals in her history, and well may her sons rejoice in their English birth; but there have been times when devils might have rejoiced and angels wept at the deeds done by Englishmen, and the day of the sack of San Sebastian was one of them.

After a short stoppage we proceeded onwards again through sombre gorges, rocky defiles, and verdant valleys. We swept across dry and arid plains, with the long line of the retiring Pyrenees bounding their horizon, and past wonderful old villages, mostly in ruins, built in the chinks and crannies of rocky mountains, and inhabited by wild-looking men and women. The plashing rain descended and the wind whistled as we dashed through the spume and mist, with great rocks, old castles, and majestic trees looming in the midst thereof like uncouth ghosts. Then—

"One long last peal of thunder,

The clouds are cleared away;

And the glorious sun once more looks down

Upon the dazzling day."

When light once more shone on our path, we looked up and beheld high overhead beetling crags and detached boulders of rock, suspended apparently so insecurely that a breath might dislodge them from their lofty shelves, and dash them down in ruin upon the passing pigmies beneath. On that spiring pinnacle sits a mouldering castle, where Roderick, last of the Goths, transported the lovely La Cava, who cost him his sceptre and his life.

The plains of Vittoria at last appeared spread before us, indistinctly seen in the darkening twilight, with a lunar rainbow hanging over them.

Oh! the oppressive heat of Spain! Oh! the suffocating and sultry air! But the Spanish climate is often subject to great changes, and we can only say right glad were we that we took a fool's counsel, viz., our own, and had brought no end of wrappers. Like Job, we had our comforters, and fortunately had carried with us a stout great-coat to this broiling land!

FOOTNOTE:

[2] Man is naturally a benevolent creature.—ANTONIN.

CHAPTER IV.

BURGOS.—THE FONDA DEL NORTE.—THE ODOUR OF SANCTITY.—SPANISH CHARACTERISTICS.—SCENES IN THE STREETS.—THE CONVENT OF LA CARTUJA.—TOMB OF JUAN AND ISABELLA.—THE CASTLE.—THE CID.—THE CATHEDRAL.—HOW PRIESTS MAKE MONEY.

WE arrived at Burgos in the midst of a hurricane of piercing wind—wind that was more easily felt by us than it will be understood by our friends in England, who cling to the obstinate notion of the incessant heat of Spain. The cold of that October night, far more intense than an ordinary mid-winter night in England, was made more severe by the utter absence of all comforts, and by the piteous appearance of the natives who shiver and shake all over the country, rolled up into peripatetic bundles of drapery, like denizens of frozen regions. There are people who leave off fires and flannel waistcoats in England because it is the first of April, although, snow may be on the ground; and we have no doubt that several of our friends would have had us array ourselves in white jane pantaloons and linen jackets because we were in Spain. No, there is no reason that, because a man is clever and *au fait* at all that concerns that state of life to which God has called him in the British metropolis, his meteorological and thermal assertions respecting other countries are to be believed in unreservedly by his friends.

Meanwhile, "Burgos!" was suddenly shouted by the guard of the train, and on looking out, we found we had arrived at that station. About a mile off was the great cathedral, so well portrayed by our David Roberts, looming before us ghostly in the dim light of the watery moon. We descended on to the platform half asleep, and anxious about the portmanteaux, while the train whisked off, leaving us alone, like stranded mariners on an unknown shore. We looked about us, and saw uncouth figures gliding about here and there with lanterns gleaming in the darkness, shapeless forms wrapped up to the eyes in dirty coloured blankets—their heads extinguished with steeple hats and other romantic and curious gear.

A small crowd gradually gathered around us as we sat upon our pieces of baggage, like Marius among the ruins of Carthage, and then everybody began to talk at once with the most frightful velocity and alarming gestures. The chorus, not very unlike that of evil demons in some weird opera, continued for several minutes, raging with great vigour and such rapidity that we could not make even the wildest guess at their meaning, because, amidst the babel no words of their patois could be distinctly singled out.

However, directed we suppose by the special providence which presides over British tourists, we eventually made a desperate resolution to follow our luggage and cling to it to the last. Following these tactics, we found ourselves in a short time seated in an elongated vehicle, innocent of all springs, which had some resemblance to a schoolroom on wheels, with all the candles put out. In this conveyance we had the further advantage of the uninterrupted society of a monkish gentleman with sandals, cowl, rope, and what seemed to be a long hairy dressing-gown. Now, we have often heard of the odour of sanctity, but if the odour by which this holy person was accompanied was the article in question, we must say we didn't think much of it.

The vehicle in which we were seated started with a shout, a crack, and a jerk, very suddenly, and, to any one a little absent, without sufficient warning. After rattling over the most fearful pavement, past grey, gaunt buildings, and through dark, narrow, shadowy streets, illuminated at long intervals by a misty lamp swung across from house to house, we were landed at the door of the Fonda del Norte.

At this juncture, the fact that in this life confidence in things as they should be, instead of suspicion of things as they are, is a mistake, was forced upon us very decisively; for had we, on descending from the omnibus, not considered it natural that there should be a step upon which to place the foot, instead of regarding it as possible that there might not be one,—especially if it was at all required,—we should not have fallen heavily out into the road, and been smeared all over with dirt and mire.

After holding out a handful of small coins, thus simplifying matters by letting the omnibus-driver help himself, we were escorted in slow procession,—the luggage going first,—by a train of four damsels, and a very brown old woman, bearing candles, through winding passages all whitewashed, up cold stone flights of stairs, the walls of which seemed to be covered with any amount of black-beetles, until we were ushered into a small double-bedded room, also whitewashed, and adorned with violently coloured prints of saints and martyrs, with what appeared to be fireworks fizzing and exploding out of the backs of their heads. We were then presented with a cup of some darkly red and rather muddy-looking fluid called chocolate, highly flavoured with what to us is the most nauseous thing in the world,—cinnamon. A piece of black bread, and a pat of something which might once have been butter, but now resembled railway wheel-grease, or cheese, was then given to us. Half of a cold bird, of a species, we should imagine, nearly extinct, seemed as little calculated to please the appetite as the bread, butter, and chocolate. These luxuries were placed upon a chest of drawers, there being no table; and as no chair could be found of sufficient altitude to raise us to a proper level with these delicacies, we were constrained to stand at our feast.

The procession of curious followers had now halted, and deployed into a semicircle around us, doubtless to watch the effects of this astonishing banquet upon our weak minds and empty stomachs. To taste of the half-bird was at once to come to the conclusion that the poultry in Spain is fed chiefly on gravel. The black-eyed young ladies who lingered round us wonderingly while we were regaling ourselves, as if we were two specimens of some remarkable race of men, or inhabitants of the planet Jupiter dropped into their hotel, were at length swept off tittering by the brown old female, and we were left alone with the pyrotechnical saints, the whitewashed walls, a couple of iron bedsteads, two chairs, and the chest of drawers, which still groaned beneath the weight of the remains of the viands that had formed our initiatory banquet in the land of Spain. The wild cry of the watchman moaning through the narrow, silent streets, the distant clang of the great cathedral bell sounding the hour, and the misty moonlight streaming through the casement, gave a peculiar finish to our novel experiences of men and things; and so to bed—to a sleep confused with all sorts of impressions, blurred and running into each other on the palette of the mind.

Here we were in Spain; Spain, the land of historical memories—Iberian, Celtic, Phœnician, Greek, Carthaginian, and Roman. From the Phœnicians sprang Cadiz, Seville, Malaga, and Cordova. From the Greeks, Rhodians, and Zanteans, arose Rosas in Cataluña, the populations of the Balearic Isles, and the immortal Saguntum (Murviedro), which heroically resisted Hannibal, and caused the second Punic war. From the Carthaginians, who conquered Southern Spain (B.C. 237), sprang Carthagena, and also Barcelona. All Spain fell beneath the Roman yoke, and continued under it for a period of four centuries.

Spain, the land of historic memories, Gothic, Moorish, French, British; the land of the Cid and of chivalry; the land of the Inquisition and of bigotry, of the religious monster, Torquemada, [3] and of the great and cruel Duke of Alva; the land of the conquerors of Mexico and Peru, of Cervantes, Lope de Vega, and Calderon; the land of Velasquez, Murillo, and the Ideal, not to speak of extortionate hotel-keepers who are much attached to the Real; [4] the land of impecuniosity, bigotry, intolerance, and fleas; the land of love and revenge, mantillas and stilettos; the land of plenty and horror, gazelle-eyed women, and the blue cholera; the land of bull-fights, cigarettes, blue blood, beggars, monks, and dinners cooked in oil; the land of the wondrous architecture of the sombre Goth and sensuous Moor; the land of a corrupted and vicious court—of lounging, intrigue, procrastination, and pride; the land of staunch, changeless, and noble characters, and of pure and chivalrous hearts; the land of the vine, orange, and cypress—of purple mountains and dreaming sea; the land of light and shadow, of love and hatred, glory and gloom;—in fine, the land of a sensitive, generous, warm-hearted, and graceful people, but the worst government in Christendom.

We are in Spain, certainly; but how cold and sepulchral a city Burgos is! It is chill and damp, and subject to violent attacks of wind, being situated on an elevated, exposed, and treeless plain, 3075 feet above the level of the sea, and surrounded by a wide Arabian-like yellow desert, which, however, waves one vast sea of corn in summer, for it is the granary of Spain. It is sepulchral because, for all the purposes of an advanced and enlightened age, it is a buried city; and there is nothing a Burgolese hates so much as improvement. We are many hundred miles south of England; but how much more bleak and inhospitable is the climate than that of our temperate Northern isle; and we can well understand the proverb relating to the weather in this place, "*Diez meses de invierno y dos de infierno.*"

Burgos is, as we have said, much behind its time. There is no particular trade, excepting in the simple articles considered necessary for the population. The hotels are but second-rate, and are used chiefly as eating-houses for the higher class of tradespeople. Few foreigners seek their shelter.

As the morning broke we were favoured with a glimpse of the sun, which cheered us with its vivifying beams for about one hour, and then the dull leaden clouds once more passed over the face of day, while the cold winds swept down from the bare and dusty hills overlooking the town. However, as one wanders through the quiet old streets, one experiences a feeling of indolence which is soothing after the busy roar of other cities. The various colouring of the quaint Spanish streets, with the picturesque irregularity of the houses, as looked at in perspective, is light and lively. The appearance of the balconies, coloured matting, and painted shutters and blinds, is pleasing to the eye of the stranger from its novelty. There are never too many passengers to mar the repose of the scene; and on such as glide quietly past us we look with no small degree of curiosity. How interesting it is to see the good priest with the shovel hat, long black skirts, and stomach-buckle of "Il Barbiere," politely saluting the olive-coloured young lady with the graceful mantilla as she sweeps along with natural and queen-like dignity!

However offensive may be some of the sights we see in this country, however reluctant may be many of its fair denizens to part with their birthright of dirt, there is grace everywhere—grace innocent of the slightest attempt at effect, or of the smallest appearance of affectation; natural indigenous grace, worn by all, either in manner, dress, or bearing, from the highest to the lowest in the land. Even the vermin-hunting beggar, sunning his idle self beneath the carved church door, can be graceful in his rags; and an old rug flung loosely around his form, with the folds caught up here and there, and falling in an easy and becoming manner from his shoulder to his feet, gives to his figure, as he paces calmly by, an air of dignity rarely to be met with elsewhere; while the worn broad-brimmed velvet sombrero, jauntily poised on the coloured napkin which is bound round the head and falls in a knot on the nape of the neck, completes the well-known picture of the proud but beggarly Don, and places him *in propriâ personâ* before our eyes.

At every turn the eye may fall upon beautiful old gems of Gothic architecture, quaint and solemn old houses, carved with heraldic blazonry, or with statues of illustrious warriors dead ages ago set in their walls. Column, pillar, and arch are so intertwined and twisted in all directions, that the buildings look as if they had been suddenly paralysed whilst writhing all over in a fit of agony. One may pass under some beautifully fretted arch, and find oneself within a ruined court of the most graceful Saracenic device. No step breaks the sleepy silence of its light arcades; some goats only are quietly cropping the rank grass amongst the broken pavements of its great square; and the clouds are passing on softly above.

In the outskirts of the town we observed some massive yellow walls, with noble Gothic arches and windows, deep and barred, standing all alone amidst the dust of this arid climate, and looking upon the barren hills in the distance; but there was no living soul to attest whether they were convent or prison. Here and there, too, some rich relics of ancient sculpture were seen built up amidst the bricks of a barn or storehouse—the tottering Past nursed in the arms of the strong Present! In and around the city, feudal towers, grand old gateways, and the palaces of ancient nobles, of the old constables of Castile, with their *façades* ornamented with wonderful devices, armorial bearings, and heraldic monsters, are frequent objects of interest to him who can read a country's history in its antiquarian remains. From the eminence on which is built the convent of La Cartuja, situated about two miles from the city, a general view of Burgos is obtained, with the lace-like pinnacles of the Cathedral spiring to the skies, surrounded on all sides by the desolate hills and far-stretching Sahara-like plains, with scarce a patch of verdure for the aching eye to rest upon in any direction. We, in a weak moment, hired a *calèche* to convey us to the convent; but as the road thither was over the most harassing ground, now following the track of a watercourse strewn with great stones, then across level ground in which we sank up to the axles in white dust, we came to the conclusion that, like the man in the sedan-chair when the bottom came out, if it were not for the honour of the thing, we might just as well walk. Indeed, we might as well have owned to walking at once,—walking ostensibly, for though the carriage of honour was by our side, we really had to walk half the way.

Upon arriving at the gloomy portal of the convent, with its yellow walls, grated windows, and strong buttresses, upon which the long weeds were waving in the blast like the wild straws in the head of some melancholy maniac, we lifted a heavy knocker, and with it produced some blows which sounded dismally and preternaturally loud amidst the silence within. In answer to our summons, a cavernous, lean, pale face appeared for a second or so at a grating to inspect the intruders, and our exterior probably attesting the fact that no danger was to be apprehended from us, the heavy door was swung open by a poor dilapidated son of religion, in a long serge gown and sandals, who looked so depressed and shy with life-long dulness and superstition, that it was no wonder he could not lift his eyes higher than the knees of his visitors. We then entered an elegant little church with pointed arches, of the florid Gothic style, beneath a *façade* emblazoned with the arms of Castile and Leon. In the midst of the subdued light of the holy place, there suddenly broke upon us the magnificent tomb of Juan II. and Queen Isabella of Portugal, formed of white marble. It is truly wonderful that in the recesses of these lonely and decaying walls, in this forlorn spot of earth, inhabited only by five wretched and poverty-stricken monks, are seen objects of interest which, in their marvellous beauty, are unequalled, perhaps, in the world. Executed in pure Carrara marble, octagonal in shape, and raised about six feet from the pavement, with a circumference of nearly thirty-six feet, the tomb of Juan and Isabella perfectly tortures the eye by the amazing intricacy of its detail. Sixteen lions, bearing the royal escutcheons, stand in pairs at each angle; groups of innumerable statuettes, each individual a masterpiece of itself, appear resting under filigree canopies, and within a perfect network of marble lace of infinite delicacy; while festoons and bowers of feathery foliage, fruits and flowers, support birds and insects treading in their marble imagery with the springy touch of life. The statues of the royal pair lie side by side, robed in drapery which might be the finest needlework were it not stone.

In a recess in the wall near by is another wonderful tomb of the same profuse ornament and delicate finish, that of Don Alonzo, son of the above. Over the high altar is a *retablo*, a mass of gorgeous gilt woodwork representing angels sitting on very solid clouds, while whole coveys of little winged cherubim, with very red cheeks, hover round the great central figure of Christ hanging on the cross, and surmounted by a pelican tearing her breast to feed her young. The entire height of the *retablo*, from the kneeling figures of the king and queen below to the summit of the topmost clouds amidst which the Assumption of the Virgin is represented, must be nearly forty feet. The gilding with which this magnificent work is profusely adorned, is said to be part of the gold brought by Columbus from America. The finely-carved walnut-wood stalls of the choir are specimens of the wonderful industry and exquisite taste of olden times, and a characteristic of all Spanish churches.

In the central ground of the silent convent cloisters the rank weeds wave over some hundred graves of Carthusian monks. As time rolls on the weeds rise higher and tangle thicker, but the stoneless mound gradually sinks down to the general level of the earth. However worthy the actions or great the deeds of the poor, their graves are ever silent, their names are but writ in water, and the very grass above them withers not so soon as their memory.

After having seen everything that attracted our curiosity, we returned through the deep white dust, and over the stony tracts, with our very useful vehicle jolting behind us, the coachman wrapping more closely round him his ample garment,—a garment with considerably more pretension to hair than to shape, being composed of the skins of many goats. I suppose he rarely, if ever, took it off, night or day; and it is probable, if he ever ventured to dispense with a vestment which had become almost a part of himself, he might have felt the consequences of his rashness.

We fear it is our painful duty to remind the reader that Burgos and the Duke of Wellington were once associated together. Glory is a fine thing, but it is apt after a time to become a *bête noire* to many excellent readers; however, that is their look-out. In November, 1808, Burgos became the head-quarters of Napoleon. Wellington, fresh from his victory of Salamanca, invested the town; but, in consequence of the insufficient support of the Spanish general, was compelled to raise the siege in order to escape being captured by Marshal Soult, who was approaching with an enormous force. To join Hill was the Duke's necessary object, as his troops were few in number, badly provisioned, and worn out by a continued struggle against great odds and many disadvantages, the little band having with them to carry on the siege but three field-pieces and five howitzers, against twenty-six of the French. After a loss of two thousand men, the retreat of the English was carried out with much hazard; but in June, 1813, the fortune of war was changed, and King Joseph, upon the approach of the Duke of Wellington, evacuated the citadel, after blowing up the fortifications, and with them several hundred Frenchmen.

In the Castle at Burgos, once a sumptuous palace as well as a citadel, the marriage of the Cid took place; also that of Edward the First of England and Eleanor of Castile. Burgos is illustrious among cities, as having given birth to the Cid, who in 1040, first saw the light in a house which stood on the spot where now stands an obelisk, in the Calle Alta, erected by Charles III. in 1784. There are, of course, a large number of people who know all about the *Cid*, and the derivation of the word. But as we are equally certain there are a fair amount who do not, we may as well mention the following particulars in connection with that semi-mysterious personage, to whom frequent allusions are unavoidable in a book about Spain.

Don Rodrigo Diaz de Bivar, otherwise the Cid, was a gentleman of very warlike tendencies, and spent most of his time in giving vent to the martial ardour within him. He has consequently been regarded by his countrymen of all times as their national hero, and wrapped in a bright haze of fabulous glory and fame. He, however, accomplished a good deal of the work attributed to him, and chased, harassed, conquered, and imprisoned the Moors throughout Spain to a most satisfactory extent. His love for the beautiful and heroic Ximena exemplifies the adage that none but the brave deserve the fair, and shows his prowess in the bowers of Venus as well as in the field of Mars. Shortly after his death a grand poetical glorification of his exploits was offered to his manes in the "Chronicle of the Cid;" and another, a very long time after, by the immortal Corneille in his masterpiece of "Le Cid." Upon the occasion of a great victory, some Moorish notables came to the hero and prostrated themselves at his feet, saluting him with the title of *Seid Campeador*, or Champion Prince—whence the appellation *Cid*.

Valencia was the last Moorish stronghold which fell to his arms; and there, after hanging up his spurs and horse-bit upon the Cathedral wall, where they remain to this day, he died in the year 1099. Any inquiring traveller may now satisfy the combined bent of a historical and anatomical mind by inspecting within a wooden urn in the Town Hall of Burgos, the bones of the immortal Don Rodrigo and his lovely Ximena.

Only to see the Cathedral of Burgos would amply serve as a grateful end to a pilgrimage from the uttermost parts of the earth. Coming suddenly from round the angle of some narrow street, there bursts upon the eye that glorious Gothic pile, with all its airy pinnacles. In the interior how rich is this majestic temple with that unequalled pomp so significant of the Roman Catholic faith, while the solemn walls are fretted with chaste ornaments of the rarest beauty, and with groups of slender, graceful pillarets which rise arrow-like to the lofty roof. When one views it, as Scott recommends us to view Melrose, in the pale moonlight, how profound is the impression produced by the weird-like appearance of the immense building, the design of which is so noble, so perfect! The awed pilgrim from other lands, when his eyes first rest on this unequalled shrine, stands enchanted, as if rooted to the spot, his soul leaping within him, transported with the beauty of so rare a spectacle.

As the great carved door swings back behind us, and shuts out from the senses the glare of the Spanish day, the head is instinctively bowed, and the knee bends in worship; for everything in this consecrated temple of the Divinity is calculated to excite the spirit of adoration, and to raise our faith heavenward. When we stand silent on the threshold of that holy place, beneath the lofty arches of the vaulted roof, supported by rows of colossal columns melting away into the distance; when we slowly pace the long aisles, with the tombs of the mighty dead on each side; or when we kneel with the devout worshippers before the altars in the various chapels, gemmed by hundreds of star-like lamps, the soul feels the reality of things unseen; while with the deep diapason of the organ, blended with the holy song of bands of choristers, its aspirations mount like clouds of incense to heaven. Never shall I forget the profound impression which I experienced when, in that noble fane, I felt that religious faith was at once the grandest and the most genuine growth of the human soul.

The staircase, which descends in graceful curvings from the altar to the marble floor beneath, with great griffin heads terminating the balustrades, is very beautiful, and was much admired by our own David Roberts. How magnificent, too, is the choir, with its two hundred stalls, adorned with spires, which are ornamented with the richest and most minute carving! The dark walnut-wood is all chased, chiselled, and traced from pinnacle to floor with one mass of amazing ornamentation, amidst the intricacies of which the sight loses itself, and becomes dim. The choir is entirely surrounded by tall brass railings of exquisite workmanship; and in the fifteen chapels, each enclosing objects of marvellous interest or beauty, the altars are supported by jasper pillars and columns of rarest marbles, while the *retablo* rises to the roof—a perfect labyrinth of gilt wood-carving, crowded with subjects of wondrous device. On a shelf in a sacristy is mouldering away into chips a great wooden chest which belonged to the Cid, for the indulgence of looking at which not very remarkable article of this hero's outfit a priest did not charge us more than a shilling a head.

FOOTNOTES:

[3] In the course of sixteen years, Torquemada, first Inquisitor-General of Spain, committed to the flames eight thousand eight hundred victims.

[4] About twopence halfpenny. The real is the basis of the whole monetary system of Spain.

CHAPTER V.

AGAIN ON THE RAIL.—VALLADOLID.—THE FONDA DEL SIGLO DE ORO.—THE COLEGIO MAYOR DE SANTA CRUZ.—CONVENT INTERIOR.—CHAMBER OF HORRORS.—COLEGIO DE SAN GREGORIO.—THE CATHEDRAL.—SPANISH CHARACTERISTICS.—THE THEATRE.—USE OF TOBACCO.

AS the train moved away from Burgos, the city and the great cathedral melted away from our sight, and we glided over the wide African-like plains and dried-up watercourses, past the stony hills which, extending to the far horizon, reflected the dazzling rays of the sun. Not a blade of grass or sprig of green was there to refresh the eye of man, or for cattle to ruminate on. No wonder the butter of the country is made of lard, or the milk we drink taken from the mare!

At a little station where the train stopped, an old lady, closely hooded in black serge, and looking like the popular representation of Old Bogey, entered our carriage, together with a monk. Where they came from it was impossible to conjecture, as there was no sign of village or habitation within sight of this very purposeless station in the desert. They were attended, however, by the usual escort in vogue in this country, a portion of which immediately leapt upon us and bit us. The poor insects had made but a scanty meal of their innutritious monk, and came to us for their *chasse café*, or rather *chasse moine*.

We arrived in the evening at Valladolid, once the capital town of Spain. Indeed, in spite of its position in the centre of a wide, wind-swept, sandy plain, which causes the city to be the sport of a chronic simoom, it seems to be a capital town still. For trade and agriculture the situation appears convenient, for, wonderful to say, they have got some water amidst the *tierras de campos*, which consequently yield abundant produce; added to which, the river Duero connects the city with the Atlantic—in a rather difficult and spasmodic manner, however—and the railroad maintains its commercial relations with the south and north. The name of Valladolid is supposed to be derived from the Moorish Belad Walid, or land of the Walid. This may be, however, as "our bore" said at the *table d'hôte*, "inwalid," and not to be relied upon.

In the Plaza Mayor of this city, the great Alvarez de Luna, "Spain's haughty constable," was beheaded. "Uneasy lies the head that wears a crown," and how uneasy must sit the head that trusts in princes, especially old princes who marry young queens, for all sense of honour, justice, and gratitude seems to walk out of the door when uxoriousness comes in at the window.

Here, in 1506, Columbus departed this life, and Philip II., the fortunate possessor of our sweet queen, Mary of England, came into it on May 21st, 1527. Here, in the sixteenth century, *auto-da-fés* and periodical bonfires of heretics were kept up with great spirit,—one being under the especial patronage of the above-mentioned blessed monarch, upon a scale of unprecedented magnificence. Here, Cervantes lived and wrote, and here, we regret to be obliged to add, the Duke of Wellington made his public entry, and took up his residence in the bishop's palace.

The *Fonda del Siglo de Oro*, although rather ambitious in its choice of a name, is a tolerable house enough, and the provision for the necessaries of life is not quite so primitive here as at Burgos. As regards that essential element of civilisation, the bath, the Spaniard seems still proudly wrapped in primeval darkness. On the morning after our arrival at the Hotel of the Golden Age,—where one would think all would be surrounded by pure delights,—the egregious desire for a bath took possession of us as usual; but, as in other places, we had some difficulty in obtaining that refreshing article. We pull the bell, the waiter appears; we utter the word "baños," in a low and rather humble tone, as if knowing it was vain to expect a favourable reply. The waiter inquires, "Caliente?" We answer, "No, frio." "Frio!" screams the waiter, with blanched visage, and instantly disappears like a harlequin through a trap. Presently, however, he reappears with another waiter, both looking as scared and uncomfortable as if they expected to be cross-examined at a coroner's inquest as two suspicious witnesses connected with our decease. Again we venture to ask timidly for "baños." Both waiters exclaim, in a tone of helpless amazement, "Frio?" to which query we reply in the affirmative by a nod, and they withdraw, muttering and gesticulating all down the stairs. The Spanish pathologist observes that the fit of hydromania generally attacks the Englishman between the hours of eight and ten.

In a few minutes, after a deal of scuffling outside the door, the two waiters appeared again, followed by the landlord, his wife, and a strange gentleman, carrying between them an object which had some resemblance to the state-chair of St. Peter in the basilica of that name at Rome. When this ponderous piece of furniture was settled in the middle of our room, we discovered that the seat had been removed, and a square tin pan fixed beneath, containing about two pints of brown water. Into this we madly plunged, and although perfectly sober at the time, imagined we were enjoying a refreshing sponge bath. However, this sort of thing is one of the *cosas de España*, so we suppose it was all right.

À propos of the general wonder expressed at any one wishing for cold water to wash in, there seems in Spain to be an equal terror of fresh air. Upon one occasion we had been in bed but a short time when a waiter entered the room to inquire if Señor had all he required. His eyes had no sooner rested upon the open window, which admitted the clear night air, than his whole countenance became locked and rigid, as if some dreadful personage—the travelling prophet of Khorassan, it might be—had suddenly presented himself at the window. The functionary in question, however, soon recovered his presence of mind, and having cast one anxious glance at our bed, to satisfy himself that all was right with us, he flew across the room with a bound and an oath, slammed the casements together, and the shutters after them, flinging the cross bar into its socket with such force as to show that he intended it to remain there.

The hotels in Spain, in the larger towns, are generally clean and well kept; though some persons, perhaps, might be able to dispense with a little of that universal odour of onions and ammonia which constantly prevails throughout the house; and the goods and chattels of travellers in the various rooms would not be absolutely endangered if common beggars from the streets were prevailed upon not to spend quite so much of their time on the stairs between the bed-chambers and the ground-floor.

Valladolid being a town of considerable importance in the history of Spain, we were eager to see it, and were soon threading our way through the sunny streets, underneath the broad band of blue overhead, until we found ourselves face to face with the Colegio Mayor de Santa Cruz, a grand old palace founded by Cardinal Mendoza in 1479, and now standing with all its beautiful fretwork clogged with wild weeds, and its light arcades, Saracenic columns, and Gothic porches mouldering away in sun and silence. On we wandered, through the long galleries, till we reached the library, apparently so called on account of the total absence of books, but which is filled with a mine of wealth in the shape of a profusion of specimens of the most exquisite carvings in walnut wood and dark oak. There are *salas* after *salas* filled with old musty pictures, carvings, and wooden sculptures, collected from the various convents at the period of their suppression. The pictures are mostly bad, though many of them are curious. Of course there are numbers of hoary old saints in rags, with gold quoits fixed on to the backs of their heads, glorifying in the lying label placed beneath them. A long room is filled with fearful painted figures carved in wood, representing troops of gigantic ruffians in the act of persecuting Christ, more grotesquely hideous than anything we could imagine in our worst dreams. Is it in order to inspire a due reverence and affection for Our Saviour that the figure of the Redeemer is represented in these productions as a meagre, wan, and emaciated skeleton of a man, covered all over with blood, dirt, the marks of stripes, and tangled masses of real red hair? or is it to render more intense the dislike with which we regard his persecutors? These individuals are represented belabouring their unfortunate victim with cudgels considerably larger than their own bodies, which have the most revolting appearance from deformity and disease, enormous tumours being generally appended to their throats.

In the midst of these delectable horrors, and placed on a large plate, is a painted wood-carving of the decapitated head of St. Paul, with which any amateur executioner may regale himself to his heart's content. So faithfully rendered is the last look of horror in the half-closed glass eyes, that one cannot help doubting, when he first glances at it, whether it is only a model. We were glad to escape from this religious Madame Tussaud's into the bright sun and open air, where we could dismiss the fancies inspired by such horrible sights.

We felt quite relieved when we found ourselves again in the great square, alive with dark-skinned men and women, with their gay dresses and sonorous voices. The jingling mules even were a pleasant sight to us, and we gazed with delight on the white walls, reflecting with such dazzling brilliance the rays of the sun, and on the universal dust, which almost half choked us, not to speak of the blue sky and the green acacia trees. In fact, the very odour of garlic was not so detestable to us as it used to be. Certainly those vast, prison-like convents standing on the outskirts of the town, are most fitting places in which to immure for life young men and women—fitting for their purpose, that is, inasmuch as there is nought to be seen from the grated windows to tempt them back to the world they have left. They may strain their dimming eyes as much as they please through the bars, they will see no stirring crowds in pursuit of business or pleasure, no happy pairs, no manly form or sweet face, to make the still warm heart thrill with joyful memories; they will see nought but wild tracts of desert, and yellow plains fading into the hot horizon, and spreading away like a burning ocean. We have by chance upon rare occasions caught sight of faces at convent gratings, and their glance fell like an icicle on the heart—faces which, though young in years, were aged in sadness, and perchance with the remorse—most probably with the regret—that comes too late. I saw, on one occasion, two young girls, pale from confinement within the yellow walls of a religious prison at Valladolid, and the bloodless cheek rendered the dark blaze of the gazelle-like eyes almost unnaturally bright with a false lustre, the lustre caught from the soul loosened by the partial decay of its prison-house, and struggling to be free. How strange that so much young, ardent life, so much beauty, so many loving hearts, and so much generous energy should choose to rot uselessly away in such prison-houses, like pale and lonely lamps flickering in a tomb! Strange that their mission as tender women, who might have soothed the griefs and tempered the hardness of many an honest man, who in return might have loved them as his life, his pride, his all, should be—as citizens of the world—tied to a destiny so awfully aimless, hopeless, and loveless: so dead in their life, and in only too many cases so utterly heart-weary and forlorn!

Well, to proceed with our stroll through the picturesque old Spanish streets. We say Spanish,—for it is not every town even in Spain that is Spanish in the character of its architecture. Madrid, for instance, with the exception of a few of the old quarters, has nothing nationally characteristic about it. The sun was now beginning to make itself felt with more than usual vigour; but that was to be expected here, for it is one of the *cosas de España*. From the yellow walls of churches and palaces, its rays were reflected, while overhead there hung one spotless lake of blue. Down a melancholy silent street, where lean dogs were quarrelling for offal, and fierce-eyed, ragged fowl were pecking savagely amongst the dust, was a plain square house, with a few small windows closed by shutters. In this house Columbus died, as the stranger is informed by the following inscription over the door: "Acqui murio Colon."

A little further on we came upon an avenue of dry poplars, bordering a small sluggish stream, through which was seen a telescopic view of hot, yellow hills beyond, dotted here and there with rare patches of green, as if the genius of fecundity, in flying over them, had by accident occasionally dropped from his cornucopia a huge bunch of cress. By the side of a ditch, we observed hundreds of washerwomen on their knees, washing shirts in mud, with a large stone. The chattering they made induced "our bore," whom we suddenly met on the bridge, to observe that "there seemed to be a great deal more talking about one thing and another than about anything else." What he meant, goodness knows! A little beyond, was a boy on his stomach, drinking from the stream, not, like the wolf in the fable, above the lamb, here typified by the washerwomen, but below. No wonder cholera is more than usually fatal in Spain, for, certainly, many of their practices invite the approach of pestilence!

It seems an innocent practice enough, the taking notes occasionally in a pocket-book; but here, in the Peninsula, it is rather nervous work. For example, we had scarcely finished a few lines in pencil on one occasion, when we became aware of the close proximity of two *gendarmes*, who were both looking aslant over our shoulder, into the book. For half an hour or so, they followed us persistently wherever we went, occasionally stopping and conferring earnestly together, until we feared we were going to be apprehended and thrown into a dungeon for plotting against Queen Isabel, now dethroned, and taking notes of the weak points in the character of her government and people, of which, by the way, the mode of washing linen is one.

In all the walks outside Valladolid, everything reminds us forcibly of the East, and affords evidence of the Oriental descent of the Spaniard. There is, in fact, much truth in the assertion that Spain is but *l'Afrique qui continue*. There are the same hot, white, dusty roads, bordered by feathery acacias, and giving birth to the aloe; the same brazen, dry, and wide sandy plains and stunted trees. There are many of the same flat-roofed houses, against whose dazzling walls the fig and oleander cast their shadows. There are the same brown, semi-nude urchins, shouting Arabic-sounding words and whacking mules harnessed with coloured drapery.

When we look towards the town, we see vast convent walls standing defiantly, as those of fortresses, and pile after pile of great square buildings, domes, and towers, rising against the blue, sleepy sky in all their solemn beauty. When we enter the city, and walk along the cool high streets, leaving the sultry plains behind us baking in dust and glare, the eye turns upon old palaces converted into barracks and alms-houses, and upon Moorish courts and Gothic halls, apparently tenantless of any one save flea-bitten beggars, mumbling Babel only knows what language, who crawl about, scratching themselves, half asleep, amidst princely porticoes and noble columns. Everywhere we observe groups of graceful, hooded women, men swathed in red sash, striped cloak, and yellow shirt, looking out keenly from beneath the sombrero's shade. The Spaniard seems to delight in gaudy hues. Mules are clad in gay trappings, and the houses are painted in bright colours; yet everywhere, too, we see dirt, decay, and sloth, and are repelled by abominable smells.

In our rambles we went past the *façade* of the church of San Pablo, the stone ornaments of which are like lace-work executed three hundred years ago. This, one of the finest *façades* in Castile, was begun in the fifteenth century by the Abbot of Valladolid, Fr. Juan de Torquemada, and finished by the Duke of Lerma at the beginning of the seventeenth century. We passed into the beautiful patio and court of the Colegio de San Gregorio, and walked amidst the tall spiral pillarets, supporting Gothic arches, light and lovely. We then sauntered up the rich staircase, with its carved stone balustrades, diminishing away in needle-like delicacy, and looked out upon the open court with all its chiselled galleries. Even in these beautiful structures neglect was visible. Weeds in many places covered the marble, and the smell of death seemed somehow to linger around.

To a dreamy mind, or to one which easily vibrates to a touch of poetry, it is a grand luxury to turn into those fine old churches, where the light is subdued and the air is cool, from the scorching sun and glare without. We thus, occasionally, lifted the curtain, and passed under the porch of the cathedral of Valladolid. Its enormous square Corinthian columns stand in all their granite strength, as if to outwatch the world. The colour prevailing in this church is grey and sober. There is something grand and harmonious in its huge proportions; but in its simplicity it appears more like some massive sepulchre of the past than the temple of an ostentatious religion. Scattered groups of women are kneeling before the altars, and the still forms of devotees are bending on the cold pavement. Brazen gates and lofty railings surround the choir, through which coloured figures move indistinctly, as in a dream. There is some magnificent dark oak carving. Clusters of tapers pierce through the gloom, and the melancholy chaunt of distant choristers echoes softly through the aisles. Out again into a sunny market-place, with gipsy-like women squatting on the ground, amongst the melons and tomatoes, the pots and pans. Dirty though graceful men, smoking cigarettes, and entangled in rusty cloaks, with their heads tied up in gaudy kerchiefs, are lounging about in picturesque squalor; while others in black sombrero, velveteen breeches, and jacket adorned with metal buttons, are lading great mules, decked in vivid housings. Farther on are more Moorish-looking women, with pitcher on head, resting by a fountain side; and above are little boys, perched in the belfries, clanging the church bells with hearty good-will.

The Spaniard is certainly very courteous by nature, and although generally shy of foreigners, most anxious to please them when he finds them *chez lui*, and to send them away with good impressions both of his country and of himself. We were looking, on one occasion, at some monument in the town, when two young gentlemen of finished manners suddenly addressed us by raising their hats, and after politely offering us cigarettes, requested us to oblige them by an inspection of their club. Of course we were glad to do so. This establishment, which we found to be cool and comfortable enough, consisted of a suite of lofty rooms, decorated *à la Watteau*, filled with little knots of polite young men of easy manners, all dressed very soberly in black cloth, and with remarkably tall hats of the latest Parisian fashion. Most of them were chatting, playing cards, or smoking the cigarette, around a small billiard table, with very large balls and a set of skittles in the centre. A small fireplace, recently put up, was introduced to our notice, and we were favoured with a description of its functions, which could not have been given with greater pride if it had been some grand scientific discovery intended to enlighten and benefit the world. After we had been entertained for a short time, we took leave of this society of very pleasant young gentlemen, who again took off their tall hats as we bowed to them, exchanged expressions of undying respect, and favoured us with a few more cigarillos.

Spaniards seem to be generally very accommodating persons; but they must never be hurried, and never asked twice for a light for the same cigarette. They are ordinarily reserved, and have a keen sense of private dignity; but when treated with perfect consideration, are most gracious in return. Their politeness may proceed, perhaps, from a sense of patriotic obligation more than from any serious love for your person.

The ladies possess the same characteristics, and although exacting as to formalities, are generally agreeable and good-natured. It must be admitted, however, that they are very idle, entirely lacking the quick vivacity and wit of their lively neighbours, the French. The languid blood of their Moorish ancestors, and their sultry, oppressive climate, may account greatly for the indolence which is common to both sexes.

The Gran Teatro Calderon has a very pretty interior, and is quite Parisian in appearance. When filled almost exclusively with sparkling dresses and gorgeous uniforms, it has a brilliant effect. Notwithstanding recent events, the Spanish people, when we were at Valladolid, seemed to be enthusiastically loyal. Just before the performance began, a large picture of Queen Isabel, placed in the centre of the house, immediately over the royal box, was suddenly unveiled. All in the theatre with one accord stood up, turning reverentially towards it. The gendarmes posted in various parts of the *salle* presented arms, and the orchestra played the national hymn. The performance of some never-before-heard-of opera, with a title that, to us foreigners, was incomprehensible, did not, in a musical sense, do much credit to Spanish talent. However, if the prompter perhaps had not shouted so loud all through the piece, we should have heard the singers to better advantage. As it was, there was one singular duet, at all events, between a very fat, square little tenor and a long, lean baritone, of which no adequate idea can be presented, unless it be that of a two-part song performed by some person in the agonies of death and an old hound shut up in a kennel when the rest of the pack are out hunting.

What we liked very much, at all events while on our travels, was to be able to light cigarettes at the lamps in the grand saloon. Here in Spain one smokes well nigh everywhere. Oftentimes in the middle of the *table d'hôte*, if the *entr'acte* between the courses be at all a long one, cigarettes are lighted, and thrown away after a dozen puffs or so. Now women cannot naturally dislike tobacco, for in Spain tobacco is smoked everywhere, and the ladies don't faint or turn up the whites of their eyes in pretended horror of the filthy weed. On the contrary, smoking with themselves is a favourite pastime in private, if not in public, and the ladies' apartments are often fragrant with more than a *soupçon* of that herb the odour of which was so abominable to the British Solomon. And, indeed, why should it not be so? There are many worse smells that are endured without a murmur than the fresh aroma of pure Havanna tobacco, King James's Counterblast notwithstanding.

After the before-mentioned exhilarating duet, we thought that for the first dose we had better not exceed or try the human system too much; for, like the people who can in the course of time and practice take as much laudanum as would kill an ox, there was no knowing what we might be brought to endure. We strolled, therefore, into the Teatro Lope, where a farce "was on," as they say in dramatic phrase. The sources of amusement—the characters, plots, and style of playing—appeared to be pretty nearly the same as they are in England. There were, as on our stage, heavy fathers, walking ladies, housemaids, lovers concealed in cupboards, rejected suitors favoured by stern parents, but suffering much from the practical jokes of the faithful groom of the family, all shaken up together into a confused plot, and holding hands in a row when the piece was brought to the usual happy termination. When the curtain falls, cigars are lighted, and the tobacco smoke rises in clouds, until the entire house, as well as the brains of the audience, is entirely befogged. All the private boxes at this house were thickly padded with stuffed and quilted leather, with what object it was difficult to conjecture. The orchestral arrangements were conducted upon rather a *laissez aller* principle; and the boy who played the cymbals seemed scarcely to be what we should call a regular musician, but one engaged for the nonce. Being a quick-witted, sharp-eyed lad, however, he managed, by keeping his gaze steadily fixed on the leader, to play his noisy instrument with some discretion, guided by an occasional wink from that functionary. He was probably paid so much a smash, like the man with the great drum at Jullien's concerts, who received twopence per whack.

Valladolid is an exceedingly pleasant place, and we enjoyed very much this *existence de flâneur*, going about during the day from sight to sight, and passing the evening in the theatre. Indeed, when one is associated with a kindred spirit, what more charming holiday can there be than to be carried past a panorama of ever-changing scenes, and, with all care left behind with the London fogs and lawyers, to witness views of life, nature, and character dissolving one into the other by easy gradations, now light, now grave, now humorous, now gently sad? It was with equal delight that we wandered through the busy city and in the mountain breeze, under balmy skies, and over the azure sea. So, then, Valladolid, *addios*!

CHAPTER VI.

EN ROUTE FOR MADRID.—TYPES OF NATIONAL CHARACTER.—GEOLOGICAL CONNECTION OF SPAIN AND AFRICA.—A STATION IN THE WILDERNESS.—AVILA.—A FUNERAL.—THE GUADARRAMA HILLS.—THE ADUANEROS.—MADRID.—HOTEL DE LOS PRINCIPES.—PUERTA DEL SOL.

WE had the advantage of an American gentleman's society in the railway carriage when we started for Madrid; also that of a rather pedantic Englishman—both types of their respective nations. It was most interesting to observe how, by asking both the same question, the peculiarity of their separate nationalities was brought into curious contrast.

"Do you prefer the opera house at Valladolid to Her Majesty's?" asked we, in the course of conversation, of the Englishman.

"Sir," replied he, "upon the occasion of an examination at a public school, I was once requested to name the greater prophets, and then to name the less. I immediately refused, and observed to my examiner that I never made invidious distinctions. I now make you the same answer."

We then put the question to the American, who said,—

"Waal, stranger, I guess I prefer neither, for the manner in which you conduct operatics in Europe is a caution to snakes, and aside of being ridiculian in manner, I put it down slick as base and tyrannical, which howsomever is only as how yew poor Europēan crittars is suckled to enjure, except Irish cutes, who, I calculate, are absquatulating from the rotten old world, and making pretty quick tracks across the fish-pond to the Almighty States, and that's a faact."

At this juncture it seemed necessary to lead our friend back to the subject of the opera, else he would have probably dilated upon very inconvenient subjects, until, as he himself had occasion to observe, "Eternity's bell rang."

It came out, however, that the English method of conducting operatic matters was worthy only of an effete and senseless old aristocracy. In England we were assured by our independent *compagnon de voyage* that a prima donna who happened to have a bad sore throat was still compelled to sing as well as if her voice was in the best condition. Was there ever such cruelty? Notwithstanding the danger to that delicate and costly organ of song, the human throat, she was forced to come forward and execute the most elaborate and difficult airs, with variations, to amuse a public the most exacting and the least sympathetic in the world; whereas in America, if the lady's throat was at all in a delicate condition, she was at once excused by her enlightened audience, who never expected that impossibilities were to be accomplished for their gratification. In fact, according to this gentleman's account, America must be so free and enlightened a country, that it is a wonder that such old-fashioned notions as obligation, contract, &c., &c., should exist therein, or that prima donnas should ever sing at all during an opera, unless perfectly convenient to themselves. In fine, if our friend's judgment was to be trusted, the national motto of Columbia should be the accommodating one of that much respected establishment, suppressed a century ago, the Hell-Fire Club—to wit:—"Fay ce que voudras." [5]

The commencement of the journey, after leaving Valladolid *en route* for Madrid, lay through vast tracts of sandy plains, with the far horizon bounded by brazen hills like those of Africa, and long, lofty table-lands, beneath which the Nile might well be streaming. But this is indeed, at this season at all events, a dry and barren land, where no water is. However, many broad acres of this now arid country were a few months ago smiling with waving corn. Still desolation must in a great measure be the general characteristic of the scene, with Oriental-looking mountains of bare sand, on which nothing can grow but stones, and where life is rarely seen in any form save that of the wild goat, the vulture, and the outlaw. There is little doubt that, at one of those far distant epochs with which geological science makes us familiar, the two continents joined at the spot where are now the Straits of Gibraltar, and that Spain was then continuous with Africa. In point of fact, the soil of Spain, as far as Burgos, has precisely the same characteristics as that of Africa.

So on we glide, over plains and tracts of glaring sand, enlivened only here and there by a solitary peasant driving a flock of black sheep over the white expanse to places where a few miserable patches of some rank vegetation offer a meagre grazing ground for the poor animals. At long intervals there appears, seated on the plain like some low, flat island, a wretched poverty-stricken town, the burning rays of the sun reflected from its broken house-tops and off its yellow walls. In the far distance the eye may perhaps distinguish another, and after we have passed it, yet another, rising far away, isolated on the dreary waste. A large church seems to domineer over the hovels beneath, its toppling spire leaning as it were with neglect and exhaustion. Scarce a soul appears amidst these mural wildernesses. There is none of that stir, animation, and cheerfulness which generally accompany city, town, or village life in other countries. The burning sun, the sandy desert, the monotonous wilderness, have evidently left their impress on the character of the people. As we proceed rapidly over the plain, a pile of tower and battlement in ruins—a relic of heroic story, and of the glories of other days—appears before us, standing midst the solitude like the skeleton of some long-forgotten animal which had fallen there when the world was yet young, and over which now the wild birds scream and whirl, while the long, rank weeds which nearly cover it sigh to the passing breeze.

This bright October weather is like the finest July days in England, tempered by a fresh, gentle, and wholesome breeze. We stop at little stations in the midst of the wilderness; in fact, it seems that we stop pretty nearly as often as it suits the guards or engine-drivers, for the stoppages are not confined to stations or villages, but sometimes take place in the middle of fields, where there is no sign of habitation. Some woman, perhaps, may rise from the border of a ditch, where she has been resting, with a child in her arms, and all the officials will get down and have a chat with her, while the good-natured passengers, who take the stoppage as a matter of course, get out and smoke cigarettes.

When some lone station, which is represented by one small house, is reached, the carriage windows are immediately surrounded by tottering old men in ancient velvet hats with very broad brims, and with little silk balls dangling therefrom. They are all swathed in a wonderful collection of rags, pinned, sewed, nailed, and tied on to their bodies anyhow, while their legs are bound up in pieces of sacking, and their feet apparently encased in poultices. Where they come from none can tell, nor can man's ears divine their speech—some patois which even native Spaniards can hardly understand.

Amongst the specimens of drapery composing the toilet of one poor old man, whose face was simply black from dirt and sun, who seemed actually rotting alive, and who appeared to think there was nothing in his condition to regret, there were two triangular patches of green damask, with roses worked thereon, fastened somehow on to his back, together with a remnant of a sail-cloth shirt. One sleeve of the latter was of yellow cotton, while the other arm was concealed from view by a short mat of horse-hair and a piece of carpet sewn together. A sash of faded scarlet encircled his waist, and his lower extremities were enclosed in inexpressibles made of goat-skin with the hair outside. He had a long stick in his hand, and was accompanied by a lynx-like dog, who devoured greedily grape-skins as they fell from a carriage window. This poor old man had no teeth, only one eye, and was very much bent. He and the other ancients were such masses of dirt that they must have been designed by Providence as places of refuge for destitute insects.

These beggars are generally seen in small companies, and it is not advisable to approach them too nearly, as there is a deal of *esprit de corps* amongst them. Whence the poor wretches come, and where they live, no one can tell, for there is not even one of those decaying old towns, with the big church before mentioned, near their usual haunts. They seem to exist simply—because they don't die—from mere force of habit. There are beggars, of course, in all countries; but such degraded, miserable beings as we meet in beautiful Italy and brilliant Spain, are to be seen in no other part of the world.

After this purposeless stoppage, our express train moves on again at a good six miles per hour, and there is no further halt till we reach the ancient city of Avila, founded by Hercules, and the birth-place of St. Theresa. Its decaying old streets, its high mouldering castle, its Gothic houses, and its large churches, have all a very forsaken aspect. It is surrounded by great military walls, lofty, massive, and grey, [6] through which the listless-looking natives have egress from the city into the wilderness around by means of gateways of enormous thickness. There is something sad and impressive in seeing this ancient city, in which there are so many remains of power and grandeur, now given up to the inexorable hand of time and the cold blight of desolation. What a sermon might be preached from such a text on the mutability of all earthly grandeur!

As if to make the solemnity of the scene more complete, while we were sauntering during our hour's halt through the dark old streets of Avila, a funeral procession came by, preceded by a troupe of ghoul-like creatures, bearing their stiff and soul-less burden, hooded in black from crown to sole, with scarce a semblance of humanity in them, save the unholy-looking eyes, which, amidst the deep drapery, glanced furtively at us from out the cavernous eyeholes in the masks which they wore. The mournful procession consisted, as usual, of shaven priests, attendants bearing flambeaux, and children singing the Miserere; in a word, there was all the empty pageantry with which the Catholic Church deposits the dead in their last earthly home. The coffin was painted a bright crimson colour, and a key was fastened near the lock by a chain, to be in readiness at the Day of Judgment.

When we had taken our places in the train again, the steam was put on, and we moved off, gradually increasing our speed till it reached the unprecedented velocity of nine miles an hour. This greatly alarmed a lady in the carriage, who, no doubt, was of that Spanish Conservative party which prefers things as they are. People in America, even the ladies, take matters much more quietly. An ancient dame was travelling by rail for the first time in her life, and when the "smash up," which is almost a matter of course among our go-a-head friends, came, and fatigue-parties arrived to carry her off with the other wounded on a stretcher, she was quite astonished when told that it was an accident, as she had thought the whole thing a regular pre-arranged part of the business of every-day railway travelling, and took it all quite comfortably. In fact, she was rather interested than otherwise in her initiation into one of those stirring incidents which it is the fortune of travellers to encounter more frequently in America than elsewhere.

Meanwhile we glide on through dreary regions, the far distance bounded by barren mountains. We pass over vast treeless plains strewn in all directions, as far as the horizon, with huge broken masses and boulders of granite. A scene more expressive of gloom and desolation cannot be imagined. The huge fragments, scattered about as far as the eye can reach, are piled up occasionally into enormous heaps, which look like the remains of ruined cities of an unknown age; or spread widely over the grey expanse, like the tombs of the races which once inhabited these regions. It is impossible, indeed, to conceive anything more austere than the effect produced by a scene at once so grand and so desolate.

The railroad now began to ascend by gradual inclines, making wide casts over the stony tracts. The amount of engineering skill, money, patience, and gunpowder it must have taken to cut through, in some places, miles of solid granite, must have been great. We were now commencing the ascent of the Guadarrama Mountains, which overlook from afar the capital of Spain. This fine *ferrocarril*, the construction of which is somewhat similar to that of the railroad over the Sömmering Pass near Trieste, surmounts altitudes by curves and gradual inclines.

The Guadarrama Mountains, with other sierras, of which the principal are the Somo Sierra, the Sierra Morena, the Alpuxarras, the Sierra Nevada, and the Sierra de Ronda, are remarkable features in the aspect of Spain. Surrounding the plains of Castile and La Mancha, the highest of such extent in Europe, with strong natural bulwarks, they are invaluable to the Spaniard in the defence of his native land. They even seem to constitute distinct moral divisions of the inhabitants. The whole country thus appears to be formed of several intrenched camps, and is admirably adapted for a war of posts—particularly for guerilla warfare, by their skill in which the Spanish mountaineers were enabled to offer such a successful resistance to their French invaders.

Higher and higher wound the road, until we suddenly burst into a region of pine forests, which darkened the sides of the mountains. The profound gorges, the aspect of which was so savage, were rapidly filling with purple mist as the sunset left them, to fall in various tints of farewell glory upon the loftier ranges of distant mountains, which seemed to melt away, wave on wave, against the clear, far heavens. The middle ground was filled with a broad expanse of warm, rose-lit plains, from the bosom of which, at unequal distances, towered enormous rocks, clothed to their summits with pine-trees. What a prospect it was! Such a scene of mingled gloom and glory the pencil of Salvator alone could render—the funereal plumage of the deep forests waving on the mountain's side, and the long rays of the sinking sun shooting through the darkness like celestial arrows, while high above a few feathery cloudlets sailed tranquil through the liquid ether, like troops of supernal messengers.

The shades of evening were falling upon the earth, when a vast, grey edifice of gloomy majesty loomed ghostly in the twilight, resting under the shadows of a darkening mountain, and all alone amidst a region of wild and desolate grandeur. This was the Escorial, the grand convent-palace of Philip II., and the burial-house of the Spanish kings. Such an edifice, almost the vastest in the world, in such a spot, and seen for the first time at such an hour, impressed one with a feeling of wonder and awe. We had little more than a glimpse of this historical building as we glided past. Our carriage moved on, now filled with dark women with brown babies, and soldiers with white kepis and red trousers; while, of course, a dash of garlic was not wanting, with the odour of five cigarettes going simultaneously, to render unbearable the atmosphere in the carriage, all the windows of which were hermetically closed, in order to exclude the terrible fresh air.

At last, however, to our joy, Madrid was reached. Nothing could exceed the extreme polish and urbanity of the *aduaneros*, of whose severity we had heard so much. Instead of ransacking the luggage, and making hay of one's shirts, a very handsome dark young man in uniform, having satisfied himself of the truth of our statement, that we were not professional smugglers, offered us a cigarette, gave us a light from his own, took off his hat, observed that he immensely admired the British Constitution, and then ordered us a brougham. The existence of such a class of officials at a terminus is really not an unmixed good. Imagine what might have occurred had we been susceptible daughters of Albion on their travels with an invalid or sleepy mamma! We tremble for the peace of mind of future English young ladies, travellers to Madrid.

Madrid, looked upon merely as the capital town of Spain, is extremely disappointing, [7] and simply a bad imitation of Paris, with little or nothing in it of original Spanish customs or life. The street architecture is modern, garish; it has a gingerbread appearance, and the use of whitewash has been too liberal. Although in the centre of Spain there are no remains of the Moorish or mediæval periods, nothing to represent the better class of art; and if you would find a bit of downright, dirty, picturesque Spanish street, you must penetrate to the back settlements, or the St. Giles's of Madrid—in fact, to the Calle de Toledo. There, beneath a blue sky, with squatting brown women suckling naked brown babies in the sun, gaudy churches, squalid houses, priests and beggars, not to speak of fish, vegetables, offal, and dogs, you may, after removing your handkerchief for one moment from your nose, imagine yourself amongst the slums of Naples.

With the exception of some few women of the middle and lower classes, who pin black silk aprons on to the backs of modern *chignons*, and on Sunday, or at the bull-fight, perhaps a bit of old lace, none are seen wearing the graceful mantilla, or those dark robes with ample skirts that sweep the streets. The traveller has rarely an opportunity of observing in the capital that delicate and piquant flirting with the fan which we always associate with our ideas of Spanish ladies; but he may occasionally remark very bright and meaning glances directed to the opposite sex by eyes of dazzling lustre. To see the romance of old Spain, however, one must go down south to warm Seville and historic Granada, where, by the way, we do not intend to go, as everybody has been there before; and it has now become a matter of legitimate pride to be able to say: "Behold before you a man who has not been to the Alhambra!"

The men in Madrid, although sometimes wrapped from heel to nose in the orthodox conspirator cloak, make themselves very eccentric in appearance by crowning their heads with that latest invention of the Evil One, the modern French chimney-hat; and that, too, in a very exaggerated form. The utter incongruity of these two articles of manly dress must be seen and felt to be thoroughly appreciated. To a tourist, indeed, who travels at a vast outlay of time and expense—to say nothing of cheerfully delivering up his body as a pasture-ground for innumerable fleas—in order to see Spain and the Spaniards as they ought to be, it really enters like iron into the soul (although, for the life of us, we could never understand that anatomical operation), to see Spain and Spaniards, in the matter of costume, at all events, as they are, and as they ought not to be.

However, here we are, for better or for worse, safely landed at the best hotel in Madrid, on the Puerta del Sol, and we are bound to say we did not find it as a married man, on the authority of a well-known anecdote, is said to have found his wife,—all worse and no better. The Hotel de los Principes will take a deal of beating from any hotel in Europe in point of comfort, cleanliness, and civility. Situated on the sunny side of the Puerta del Sol one has the pleasure of looking on an ever-changing and busy scene below, as he smokes the morning *cigarillo* in the balcony. On this spot, in former days, according to a popular legend, there stood a church upon whose door the sun, for some mystic reason, remained long after it had left all other doors. The gateway or door of this church was consequently called *La Puerta del Sol*, from which the present *plaza* derives its name.

This open space is the life and heart of Madrid, all the principal arteries of the city proceeding from it. Here, all business is done, and pleasure taken; speculations are entered into, and politics discussed (as much as is consistent with personal security); and, consequently, it is the first place to which foreigners resort. It is the exchange, the betting-ring, and the general lounge. The garrison, with flags and band, march through it once a day; and to those who were so minded, here was the best chance, at the time of our visit, of looking upon the countenance of Queen Isabel II., as she passed in her chariot and four-in-hand of mules.

FOOTNOTES:

[5] Motto in old French, now to be seen over the Abbey door of Medmenham, near Harleyford, the seat of Sir W. R. Clayton, Bart., where the Hell-Fire Club held its carousals.

[6] Some of the walls composing the fortifications, which are a sample of the engineering skill of the eleventh century, are forty feet in height and twelve in breadth.

[7] The Madrileños, however, are very proud of their city, hence the proverb:—"*Hay una ventana en el cielo para mirar Madrid.*"

CHAPTER VII.

MADRID.—GREAT ENGINEERING FEAT.—THE PICTURE-GALLERY.—PASTIMES AND OCCUPATIONS OF THE MADRILEÑOS.—THE BATH AND TOILET.—QUEEN ISABEL AND THE KING CONSORT.—THE VIRGIN'S WARDROBE.—THE ROYAL ARMERIA.—REMARKABLE PAINTINGS.—CHURCH IN THE CALLE DE TOLEDO.

MADRID is by far the most flourishing town of Spain; and if there is such a thing as progress, artistic, political, or social, it is of course to be found therein. It suffers, however, under an unfortunate agglomerate of disadvantages, such as a river without water; [8] a great elevation in the midst of barren sandy plains, over whose treeless surface the winds are ever blowing—in summer hot and blighting, in winter with keen and piercing breath, from the snows of the Guadarrama range; streets periodically liable to showers, not of rain, but of bullets; careless government; a distrustful population; and a total want of private enterprise, which has been all but stamped out.

One hears, however, a great deal about *Progresista* ministers, who have certainly instituted various companies of credit, to which is owing the web of railways which is rapidly spreading throughout the country, and connecting the capital with the Mediterranean, the Atlantic, and the North. Drought, which was once much dreaded, is now at least rendered impossible, as a river, the Lozoya, has been conducted from twelve leagues off, amongst the Guadarrama mountains, to the city; [9] an engineering feat that the Progresistasts are never tired of bringing before the notice of the intelligent foreigner, and which the priests look upon with great suspicion, as some of the first-fruits of the great Antichrist, Civilisation, the attendant fiends on which, in their opinion, are Industry and Progress. A fountain of real water(!) now plays in the centre of the Puerta del Sol, of which the inhabitants are extremely proud.

Some of the larger buildings of Madrid are ambitious in design, but somehow they appear as flimsy as if the material used in their construction were pasteboard. The general aspect of the streets, compared with those of the old Spanish cities, with their massive and venerable buildings, is modern and paltry. There is none of that imposing magnificence which in some of the old provincial capitals seems to accord so perfectly with our conception of Spanish dignity and grandeur. There are twelve theatres, a splendid bull-ring, an enormous palace, the finest gallery of pictures in the world—for which the Spaniards are indebted to a great extent to Cromwell, who blindly sold them the fine collection which he appropriated from his king's effects after he had brought his plot for the judicial murder of Charles I. to a successful issue. In a long promenade called the Prado, the winds are ever blowing, but the flowers never; and although there are two melancholy rows of little trees, which in some measure remind one of those in a Noah's-ark, their attempts to reach anything like a decent growth, from a soil of hardened sand and stones, are singularly disheartening. Among other places provided for the amusement of the Madrileños, there is a casino, where they may play at the lucrative game of *trente-et-quarante*. Though the metropolis of the kingdom, there is no cathedral in Madrid. Some of the shops are very splendid; and to finish this rapid survey, I need scarcely mention that there is hardly a single mouth without a cigar in it, or a solitary spot that is not perfumed with the odour of tobacco smoke.

Art is here at a standstill, and the moral and material resources which raise a nation in the respect of the world are but slowly and feebly developed. Literature, which the Inquisition in past times rendered a perilous occupation, has never been able to recover the ground it has lost, and is now almost abandoned. [10] Fierce political contests and party animosities occupy all the spare time of the Madrileños; and in these the angry Dons are always ready to engage, generally with more spirit than discretion. The lounge, if not the bath, is, however, a favourite way of passing the time in Madrid, as in London. In the Prado, as in Rotten Row, one meets with some very alarming dandies, who favour one with a cold stare, as if they intended to measure him from head to foot. Yet from the best authority, as well as from our own observation, we know perfectly well that in this country, which is a very poor one, these dazzling señors and señoras find that pride has a hard struggle to maintain against poverty, and that consequently all is not gold that glitters. Although the boot is bright, it frequently contains no stocking. Although the scarf be vivid, and the pin stuck into it be gorgeous, there may be no shirt beneath. And so these beautiful Apollos, whom we behold sucking the knobs of their canes with such dignified grace, while ogling "partial beauty" over railings, may often be compared not only to whitened, but to painted sepulchres. As an illustration of Spanish manners, we have learned on good authority that an illustrious minister of government, a man of high education and taste, remained a fortnight in an hotel, and would never during that period allow the *garçon* to change the water in his washhand basin. "The farther South, the farther the bath," might well be a Spanish proverb, if it is not; and, in fact, as all geographers know, the Wash is only to be found in the North.

Now if ablution is so little practised by the higher classes, we may well ask what must be the state of the lowest? When the unsavoury truth is told, one can only exclaim with a gasp, What do they do, then? Those beautiful girls, so well *soignées*, so gaily dressed, and so fair to behold—what substitute have they for this first necessary of the toilet? "Well," we are told, "they are instructed from early youth by their medical advisers that water is unwholesome, and, as it renders the skin coarse and rugose, must be avoided. Consequently, once a week they attempt to clean themselves, as Dejazet used to do, with cold cream, a dry towel, and some white sand."

The Spaniards, in fact, are an indolent people, and have no desire to correct their slothful habits by the bracing effects of cold water; and although the great ladies, in the utter absence of all occupation, have no other task than that of fostering their beauty and pampering their vanity, they do not consider water necessary to these ends: moreover, water is scarce, and therefore dear. The medical men beyond the Pyrenees, who might be expected to correct so grave an error, are creatures of habit, conservative from force of education, and comparatively cut off from the remainder of the scientific world. The Spaniard too, besides being an hydrophobist, has always a shivering dread of fresh air. Whenever he is asked to go anywhere, it is always *muy frio* with him. And yet in spite of these customs he is not, we suppose, more unhealthy than other men.

Lounging one day on the Prado, a great clattering of hoofs was heard, and the Queen of Spain, in an open carriage, drawn by six magnificent mules, all over silver and gold, dashed past, escorted by a detachment of cavalry. By her side sat an ordinary-looking young man, who, we were informed, was the King-Consort. Every Saturday afternoon, Her Majesty visits the Church Atocha [11] to pay her respects to a coarse, black wooden doll, which is wrapped, in a very grotesque manner, in garments encrusted with gold and stiff with precious stones of sufficient value to build half a dozen hospitals and endow the poor of Madrid for life. This image, which is supposed to have been carved by St. Luke, is said to have been brought from Antioch, and popular superstition ascribes to it the power of performing miracles.

Within this church we were shown the court dress in which the Queen was arrayed some years ago when an attempt was made upon her life. It is, of course, very splendid, and the blood-stained robes were presented to the Virgin as an offering of the Queen's gratitude for her deliverance from the arm of the assassin. As the gift is repeated every year on the anniversary day, the Virgin [12] has now about as splendid a wardrobe as any modern Queen of Sheba.

While the verger, or whatever he called himself, was explaining this remarkable exemplification of his Monarch's piety, we observed that he was smoking a cigarette; upon which we, naturally thinking it was the correct thing, proceeded to do likewise. That functionary, however, put an end to our delusion at once, by observing,—

"Señor, the profane may not smoke here. I am within the bosom of the church, and my actions are consecrated."

Regarding this as one of those singular *cosas de España* to which the stranger must submit, we presented the holy, but rather dirty, gentleman with the cigarette from which our too confiding lips were so cruelly divorced.

Within the Royal Armeria are many interesting objects. Although the veneration with which we regard a sword which the hand of Cortes once upon a time touched, or a particular suit of armour in which the body of Columbus was once encased, like a jelly in a mould, may savour, perhaps, of hero-worship, idolatry, and superstition, we must acknowledge the imputation that we are subject to it. Here are the swords of Philip II. and of Francisco Pizarro, conquerors of Peru, and there that of Charles V., Emperor of Germany, together with his entire armour—the actual suit in which he was painted by Titian. Several revolvers of the seventeenth century, and a war-saddle of the Cid, are also exhibited.

For anyone who wishes to enjoy a feast of pictures uninterruptedly, and we suppose that is not an unnatural taste, the Madrid gallery is the place. Few but English travellers go there, the Spaniards seeming to care as little about the glories of their Murillos and Velasquez', as they do about Leech or Cruikshank, and perhaps not so much. There is plenty of space for the loiterer in the gallery, and in its silence he may dream away in peace a few happy hours. There are pictures here, of course, on which genius has stamped its impress, and on which all who are capable of appreciating the beauty of art gaze with admiration. That wondrous Crucifixion, for instance, by Velasquez, produces at once an impression which roots one to the spot. In the midst of a waste of lonely darkness, hangs heavily on a coarse stake of wood the dead form of the wearied man. The end of all his misery, the relief brought by death, seems to be distinctly delineated in the attitude of that forsaken, emaciated form,—with half its face veiled by the dank hair which falls over it as the head bows forward at the last mortal spasm,—a sight at which the words "It is finished" rise instinctively to our lips while we gaze at that marvellous production of perfect art. The next picture on which the eye falls is one of a brighter character—The Assumption of the Virgin, by Murillo. The look of childish, confiding innocence in the gentle face is beyond expression. As there have been inspired writers, surely there have been also inspired painters, and this Spanish master must have been one of them, during the composition of this immortal work. Close at hand is the famous picture of the infant St. John, by the same hand. Beside the beautiful boy is a gentle lamb. The little animal has crept confidingly, without a symptom of fear, to the child's side. As it should be with so pure a subject, the colouring and general treatment are nobly simple, and that is the source of its beauty.

Velasquez, of course, is represented in all his strength. Whether the subject of his portraiture be the haughty noble or the loathsome pauper, he is the quintessence of strength and truth, and the highest delineator of national character. The splendid colouring and fine *chiaroscuro* of Ribera can be recognised in several of his most beautiful productions. In the centre of the long gallery the steps are suddenly arrested before a painting which really deserves the title that the catalogue gives it—a marvel, *El Pasmo de Sicilia*, one of the masterpieces of Raffaelle. The subject is that of Christ falling under the cross; and in truth, it is a noble example of power, colouring, and harmony. The development of the human form is at once muscular and graceful, and the sufferer's sorrow is expressed with wonderful force. The grouping of the figures, most of which are nearly, if not quite, the size of life, is perfection. For force of treatment the work is a worthy rival of the Transfiguration in the Vatican, albeit the latter is celestial and mystic; while this represents the pure earthly side of Christ's nature, depicting him as a man ennobled by sorrow, untainted by sin, and purified by suffering. The expression of the Saviour's countenance, as his eyes meet those of his mother, at the moment when, smarting under blow and taunt, he faintly endeavours to rise from his bruised knees, is beyond everything that has been depicted on canvas.

Farther on, amongst this *embarras* of gems, which includes a long array of pictures any single one of which would add to a city's fame, hangs a noble Titian. Mounted (life-size) on his sturdy Flemish charger, is a grand old mediæval knight, dressed in chased and damascened armour. His round, dogged-looking head is thrust well into a simple morion, and his beard of a week's growth shows a disregard of personal foppery not unbecoming in those who make war a business, and perhaps unavoidable in the life of the camp. With stern and steady look, his long lance grasped in his nervous hand, ready to place in rest at a moment's need, he gallops towards the fray.

A *San Sebastian* of Guido, is a painting which it would be impossible to match, except by that in the capitol at Rome, by the same hand. This is, indeed, a noble picture of the young martyr. One can see by the ecstatic expression of the countenance that he is exulting in a hope that carries him, on the wings of faith, beyond the persecutions and sufferings of this world, and reveals to him the dawn of a higher, better, and purer life. What to him are the arrows burying themselves one after the other deep in his fair flesh? His soul is above, far away from pain, and in the joy of opening immortality is no longer sensible of the agonies of its earthly body.

There is a beautiful picture by Barbalunga of a dying girl. The dull grey of twilight is gradually deepening to night in the lonely chamber, and the film of death is slowly gathering on the flickering eye, symbolising the end of all that is beautiful on earth. We particularly noted one fine production by Guercino. Some wicked-looking old men are stealthily approaching Susanna bathing, creeping onward from behind with outstretched hands, as if they were going to catch a butterfly. Two naked ladies, by Titian, in his most untrammeled style, are distinctly of the flesh, fleshy; but they are splendid specimens of that great master's proficiency in delineating the human form—of his consummate fidelity to truth in colouring and expression.

The vast picture by Rubens of the Adoration of the Magi shows plainly—with many hundred others, however—how Art, *longa* as it may be, must, like all things mortal, have a limit. This limit, in the present instance, is where, the mirror being held up to Nature, Nature herself cries out with delight at her own reflection, mistaking it for another self. The limitation here attained is Perfection. We suppose that expression of adoration, as seen in the fifty faces delineated, is beyond imitation. Then how admirable is the grouping, how gorgeous the colouring, how perfect the arrangement of light and shade, never surpassed, or perhaps equalled, either by the master himself or by Titian. What an advantage to modern art it would be if we could gain some insight into the chemistry of the colours used in past centuries! Why should our Reynolds and Lawrences fade away, in some cases into mere outlines filled up with pale tints, when the paintings of the sixteenth century still retain the hues on their canvas in all their pristine splendour? The crimson drapery of one of the Magi in the picture in question seems as fresh and as brilliant as it was on the day when it was painted by the master's hand.

Of course it appears something like presumption in us to add our feeble commentaries upon the numerous gems in this matchless collection to those of the great judges who have preceded us; yet, perchance, in his simple worship of art, a little outburst of enthusiasm upon the subjects which strike a sympathetic chord within the humbler pilgrim as he passes, may be pardoned.

The great picture by Velasquez called *Las Meniñas*—The Favourites—is worthy of the distinguished reward bestowed on its painter by his patron, Philip IV. On the left, as one views the work, the great artist is seen at his easel taking the portrait of the Infanta Margarita, daughter of the king, as she stands amidst her attendant *meniñas*. The depth of the background, on which is painted the distant wall of the great oaken chamber, with a mirror in which is seen reflected the faces of Philip and his consort, is admirably given, although we are rather mystified in endeavouring to explain how persons are to be reflected in a glass when nobody is in front of it except those who are not reflected. The sombre air of the interior of the old room is truth itself. Monotony in the effect of the brown tones is saved by the distant light streaming in through an open door. On the right, in the foreground, two favourite dwarfs are toying with a large dog. The picture is a noble rendering of the domestic arrangements of Spanish royalty in the seventeenth century.

When it was finished, Velasquez inquired of the king whether anything was wanting in the work. "Yes, there is one thing, and one only," replied Philip; and, taking a brush from the artist, he traced with his own hand the red cross of Santiago, the highest order in Spain, on the painter's breast.

There are, of course, as in all galleries, no end of dead Christs and live Apostles; and also very vivid productions in the horror-line by one Goya, whose life appears to have been, besides that of an artist, court favourite, and bull-fighter, a mixture of that of Don Juan and Baron Munchausen. It would take volumes to describe half of the works worthy of high admiration contained in this richest of collections; for it holds, besides the general mass of its treasures, ten Raphaels, sixty-two Rubens', forty-six Murillos, fifty-three Teniers', sixty-four Velasquez', forty-three Titians, thirty Tintorettos, twenty-two Vandycks, fifty-four Breughels, nineteen Poussins, ten Claudes, twenty-three Snyders, fifty-five Giordanos, fifty-eight Riberas, ten Wouvvermans, *cum multis aliis.* They have been collected chiefly from the palaces of La Granja, the Escorial, and El Pardo. When it is said it is the finest collection in the world, the expression alludes more particularly to the number of actual gems and masterpieces contained therein, than to any complete chronological series of schools gradually developed before the eye.

The exterior of the gallery, or Real Museo de Pinturas, as seen from the Prado, is elegant and classic, but not too pure; and it is decidedly too long for its height.

Of course in every continental town there is always that architectural black-dose, the Cathedral, to be *done*. But, praise be to the divinity presiding over the weary Cockney, there is none at Madrid. There is nothing nearer to a cathedral than a dirty, big church in the Calle de Toledo, where we were regaled with the sight of various delectable relics: such as a saint's toe in pickle and a martyr's tooth on a velvet cushion. This church is amongst the *quartiers* of the poorer classes. It was natural, consequently, that we, poor benighted foreigners, should be supposed to be able to see, do, or understand nothing without assistance. We were, therefore, escorted all over the building by a sickly-looking old hag of a lady, who, with the one remaining tusk sticking out of her jaw like a dilapidated milestone, created sad havoc in her attempts to articulate "*la lingua dulce de España.*" What she said no pronouncing dictionary could have enabled us to interpret. She seemed particularly enthusiastic about the saint's toe, and, as she pointed it out, smiled sweetly on the side of her mouth where the one tooth was. Now, when we are shown such things as saints' toes in pickle, or the bottled tears of martyrs, we make a point of never appearing to doubt the authenticity of the same for a moment. Firstly, we assume an appearance of credulity from motives of good taste; secondly, for the reason that if the old lady who exhibits them sees one is interested in the articles brought to notice, there is no knowing what may not be eventually produced for one's delectation, even to a phial of ink which was once shown to one of our friends, in a church in Italy, as "some of the darkness which covered Egypt." We never came across anyone yet whose tongue so fairly bolted with her as this yellow old lady, who followed us like a shadow into the very streets, scratching herself with one hand, while with the other she tried to arrange into a round knot the stubble on the top of an otherwise bald head.

We that evening dined luxuriously on one of the great continental standing dishes: "Cock and Salad"—notwithstanding that the former article looked, if it did not taste, as if it had departed this life, not by violence, but from some natural disease. Being in Spain, we called for a bottle of Sherry or Xeres, the first glassful of which took us by the throat like a bull-dog and held us there. The next morning, after breakfasting at the cheerful hour of five upon tea which, when analytically considered, seemed to consist chiefly of chopped broomsticks and dead flies, we started by train for the Escorial.

FOOTNOTES:

[8] The Manzanares.

[9] The engineer, Señor Lucio del Valle, was created Marqués del Lozoya.

[10] The *Annual of Public Instruction*, nevertheless, gives a pompous list of national libraries and their contents. The number of volumes contained in those establishments is 1,166,595, spread over the capital and provinces. The library of Madrid alone contains 390,000; that of the Central University, 300,000; of Barcelona, 136,000; and of Salamanca, 55,000. There are similar institutions not only on the Continent, but in the Balearic and Canary Isles; that of Palma and Majorca contains 35,000 volumes, and that of Mahon nearly 11,000. As to the archives, the entire history of the country, of its customs and political life, may be said to be represented in them. There are 70,278 packets of papers in the old palace of Simancas, 35,000 at Alcala de Henares, 34,000 in the archives of the Crown of Aragon, and 97,000 in the national historical record office. As regards the

public instruction of Spain, there are at present 27,000 infant schools; 77 institutions for training teachers, and 5 for the deaf and dumb or blind.

[11] Antioch.

[12] The Virgin in Spain, besides having a wardrobe equal to that of a dozen earthly queens, and a collection of jewels which would take Messrs. Hancock and Emmanuel months to value, always wears a royal crown, and ranks as queen. Her household consists of the noblest and haughtiest dames in the country, and she possesses landed estates, the revenues of which are invested for the maintenance of her worship, processions, &c.

CHAPTER VIII.

THE ESCORIAL.—ITS PRECINCTS.—SPIRIT AND CHARACTER OF THE EDIFICE.—MAUSOLEUM OF THE KINGS OF SPAIN.—MELANCHOLY GUIDE.—SUBTERRANEAN PASSAGES.—ROYAL REMAINS.—CHARLES V.—PHILIP II.—THE PLAZA MAYOR OF MADRID.—QUEEN ISABELLA AT THE OPERA.

THE village in the vicinity of the great palace is called El Escorial from the quantity of scoriæ of iron which is found strewn about the neighbourhood, the *débris* of extinct iron mines. The region, from the midst of which rises the enormous mass of the second Philip's convent-palace, is very forlorn and gloomy—a spot over which we may say, figuratively, the sable wing of desolation hangs heavily. The masses of broken masonry once formed the offices of the palace which the French destroyed in war, and they now cover the sides of the barren mountains with their ruins for leagues around. The population of the rotting village, who are seething in squalor, consist almost entirely of poor beggars, crawling through the miserable rock-strewn streets, in rags which scarcely conceal their nakedness. Hungry-eyed dogs prowl, like wolves, amongst the broken walls. The whole landscape is wild and lifeless, and our glance wanders far away over lonely plains to the sad horizon, with nothing to refresh the eye, fatigued by such an expanse of grey stony regions, but forests of mournful pine, and the lofty peaks of shattered mountains in the distance, the grey giant pile of the convent itself looming in the midst like the stupendous landmark of some inexorable fate set up to outwatch the cycle of ages. The place is one of great solemnity, and one cannot approach it without feeling oppressed by its gloom; nor was that painful impression at all alleviated by the squalid and decaying appearance of the more humble human habitations in its neighbourhood, the inmates of which were equally dull, hopeless, and sad in their aspect.

The Escorial itself may be described as an enormous heap of granite formed into a tripartite whole—a church, palace, and convent. To enter into the spirit of the place the mind of the writer should be imbued with those cold and gloomy hues which characterised that of Philip II., its founder. The nature of the man, who was at once a despot and a bigot—in a word, a monarch educated by ecclesiastics—affords a key to the nature of the immense building which he reared. To be able to describe, one should feel. And here, in this vast tomb-like edifice, one does feel an indescribable awe, a sense of veneration in the contemplation of the mighty effort of the human intellect and imagination that must have been exerted in conceiving, planning, and executing a work of such stupendous proportions.

Superstition is no doubt a great evil, but it has aided in developing that spirit to which we owe some of the grandest edifices that the past has transmitted to us—some of them, dreary follies, like this, even while we admit them to be magnificent works of art. The Escorial, in fact, is the mind of Philip in stone. It exemplifies no era in art, no national peculiarities. It is the costly caprice of a man—half monarch, half monk—of a proud and bigoted spirit, too superb to forego the haughty functions of royalty, too pious not to desire to perpetuate the fame of his religious devotion to all time and generations, although devoid entirely of that quiet humility and simple piety which are the characteristics of true devotion, and place a brighter diadem on the head of kings than either crowns of gold or a vain display of sanctity.

The Escorial is said to owe its origin to a vow of gratitude made by Philip to his patron saint, St. Lawrence, on the occasion of the victory of St. Quentin, gained by him over the French, and to the constantly expressed desire of his father, the Emperor Charles V., to have a burial-house of suitable Grandeur for himself and his descendants. Approaching the building we were met by a melancholy ecclesiastic, who looked as if a glass of port wine would do him a world of good. This personage was to be our conductor through the extensive pile of buildings. We passed beneath a lofty portal into a long gloomy corridor, which seemed to dwindle away into endless distance. As we looked around and above, at the ponderous blocks composing this mountain of granite, the door closed behind us with a dull, heavy sound, shutting us up amongst the wide labyrinthine maze of innumerable passages and galleries, crossing and recrossing one another in incomprehensible order. [13] We could not help feeling at the moment as if we were bidding adieu to the world, to life, and to hope.

The passages through which we were led were often very draughty; but the vast gloomy halls were magnificent. Grim statues were arranged along the walls, and the ceilings were adorned with beautiful paintings, now fading. The staircases we ascended were so broad and colossal that they might have supported the tread of giants. We entered also some dark damp passages, on either side of which were ranged long rows of gloomy damp cells. As we followed our melancholy guide we asked him many questions, which were answered in sad tones, accompanied by sighs. Some enormous courts, open to the day, were covered with the rank weeds growing between the stones with which they were paved, as they did on the stupendous walls rising like Titan tombs around us.

We entered a huge vaulted gallery or saloon, with arched roof, and walls all ablaze with the rich coloured fancies of old painter-poets, supported by fluted columns of marble with gilded capitals, and surrounded with splendid cabinets set with jewels. These latter contain the far-famed illuminated missals and manuscripts of the Escorial. Through corridor and passage, through cloister and portal, through long suites of apartments hung with tapestry, lace, and silk, and commanding from their windows wide-spread views of the desolate plains and rugged mountains, we followed our dejected guide, ever and anon meeting his earnest glance. Passing through a low stone doorway we came suddenly into a lofty, superb, and solemn temple, supported by great granite piers, massy and solid enough in appearance to sustain the fabric of a world. When one contemplated the height of the stately walls, he could not but regard with wonder the amount of labour that must have been expended in the erection of a building of such amazing dimensions.

One of the great ends which these noble temples serve is the production of that feeling of veneration with which one cannot but be inspired when he enters their precincts. Devotion is readily kindled at such altars; and those who covered the face of Europe with these Christian fanes, knew well how they might best gather into one flock all who desired to make open profession of their Christian faith.

We next ascended a broad flight of red-stained steps, and saw before us the high altar, formed of a variety of precious marbles, and inlaid with jasper. Above it rises the *retablo*, which is supported to the height of ninety-three feet by noble columns of the four orders of architecture, and composed of red granite, precious jaspers, and gilded bronze; while beneath the broad marble platform on which we stand is the Panteon—the burial-chamber of the kings of Spain.

High up to the right is the window of the cell in which Philip died, and through which his last gaze fell upon the altar beneath, as he took a farewell glance at the marvellous church which owed its origin to him. We now approached a heavy door, guarded by the statues of Nature and Hope, the former with the inscription, "Natura occidit," and the latter, "Exaltat spes." As our monkish guide preceded us with his melancholy mien, there was something in his glance which, as if to prepare us for what we were to see next, seemed to say:—

"Keep silence, child of frivolity, for death is in those chambers.

Startle not with echoing sound the strangely solemn peace;

Death is here in spirit, watcher of the silent tomb."

The passage through which he led us was so dark and gloomy that we could follow him only by the flaring light of the torch which he carried.

We descended a long series of steps, which, as we could see by the occasional glare of the torch falling upon them, were composed of rare and precious marbles, as were also the walls of the passage itself. No gleam of daylight ever finds its way to these subterranean chambers and galleries, and it was only by the uncertain flame of the torch that we could distinguish the objects around us.

As we approached an arched gallery, we were met by a cold damp breath of air which fell icily on the brow, and told us that we were close to the Royal Mausoleum. We felt awed by the thought that we were now in the presence of all that earth contains of men who were once the mightiest monarchs of the world. The mortal remains of the kings of Spain repose in an octagonal vault, in niches rising one above another to the roof, which terminates in a sort of cupola. There are, including the queens, twenty-six bodies here inurned; and two empty urns await the present (or rather recent) queen and her mother, to whom fate will probably now deny the privilege of finding their last resting-place in the tomb of their ancestors. Two years ago Queen Isabella had the lids of all the sarcophagi removed. Profound interest was naturally felt in approaching that of Charles V., and when the form and features of the most powerful monarch of his time were found nearly intact, all who were present gazed upon his remains with mingled feelings of curiosity and awe. So little altered were the lineaments that, though nearly three hundred years had passed, they could be easily identified by those who had seen the portrait of the king by Titian. The face of his son Philip II. had shrunk greatly; but all were reported to be in good condition.

The urns are all of marble, beautifully sculptured; and the sanguine glow of the flame played on the gilded ornaments with which they were decorated. The kings are on the right of the altar, with its great gaunt crucifix, and the queens on the left, all of royal descent, in their day reigning monarchs, but now sharing the common fate of humanity. In that niche, and within that shining casket, lies what remains of him whom once the nations feared, *el César* and "Master of the World," the Emperor Charles V. Beneath, is Philip II., his son, founder of the Escorial. Within this mournful chamber the spirit of the past speaks to us, telling us how little different from that of the poorest slave is the destiny of the mightiest potentate. For the rest—"Pallida mors æquo pulsat pede," &c. Kings whose power has shaken the earth must perish, although their great influence may still throb through the globe. Subject to the common lot, their ashes are scattered on the wind, and their bodies have mouldered back into clay.

"The glories of our birth and state

Are shadows, not substantial things;

There is no armour against fate:

Death lays his icy hand on kings.

Sceptre and crown

Must tumble down,

And in the dust be equal made

With the poor crooked scythe and spade." [14]

The evening shades were falling as we emerged from the Escorial; the wild pine forests covering the mountain sides, seemed like a deep pall spread upon the land; and we looked lingeringly back on the great mass of the prodigious edifice rearing all its domes and pinnacles against the last melancholy glory of the sunset.

The Plaza Mayor in Madrid is a fine remnant of mediæval architecture, with its lofty ornamented façades, and its low dark arcades running round the square. These arcades, unfortunately, are now filled with musty slop shops, and stalls where the worst Birmingham jewellery is sold. In this immense plaza, in the year 1623, Charles I. of England—then Prince of Wales—witnessed a bull-fight in honour of his betrothal with the Infanta Maria, surrounded by all the grandees and beauty of Spain, and attended by "the profligate minister Buckingham," as good history books would call him. However, as we all know, the matrimonial engagement came to nothing, and Henrietta Maria of France was reserved for the professional attentions of the widow-maker Cromwell.

From all the country around, the square white mass of the royal palace of Madrid is seen dominating over the entire city, the immense building appearing, in comparison with the smaller houses around it, like a whale among minnows. From its terraces it commands a superb view of wide plains, stretching like a yellow sea to the Guadarrama mountains on the far horizon. It was built by Philip V., the ambitious imitator of the magnificence of the *grand monarque*, who aspired to possess a residence which should render Versailles insignificant. The building is, in some sort, a bad and most limited imitation of the Escorial, inasmuch as it covers a space of only four hundred and seventy-one feet square, and is no more than a hundred feet in height—a mere kernel for the shell of an Escorial. It possesses a chapel, courts, *patios*, no end of entrances, a perfect village of offices, and some dried-up leafless plots of ground, called by courtesy gardens. The situation is lofty, and consequently it is a veritable temple of the winds, as Her Majesty's soldiers have often experienced during the winter nights, when it was their duty to be on guard. A great *patio*, one hundred and forty feet square, surrounded by an open portico formed of thirty-six arches, and adorned with statues of various Roman Emperors,—and, we are bound to say, of some of the best of those magnates,—occupies the central part of the palace. Of course in this, as in most other overgrown domiciles of royalty, there is a grand staircase, spacious, costly, and magnificent, as described by enthusiastic sight-seers. It is constructed of black and white marble, and adorned with sculptured lions of the same beautiful stone. Upon one of these Napoleon is reported to have placed his hand, saying, "Je la tiens enfin cette Espagne si desirée." Having performed this little imitation of Cæsar's first action on landing upon the shores of Britain, he is also said to have observed to his brother Joseph—the puppet he had set up, "Mon frère, vous serez mieux logé que moi;" and then, in the character of invader, he began to contemplate with a fellow-feeling a portrait of Philip II., the husband of Bloody Mary of England, the builder of the Escorial and the projector of the Armada. Napoleon, in fact, is one of those inevitables who have left the impress of their name on almost all the cities of Europe. Thanks to history, legend, and tradition, there is nothing about the Cid at Madrid. The chapel royal, which is pseudo-classical in style, is adorned with Corinthian marble columns, and with frescoes. In our desire to see everything interesting, we visited even the coach-houses and harness-rooms, with the horse-trappings embroidered in the time of Charles V., &c., finishing with the splendid Armeria before mentioned.

We had the happiness of beholding Queen Isabella at the opera, through an atmosphere tolerably free from tobacco smoke. Her Majesty wore a wreath of diamonds, and a dress of white *moiré* silk, overlaid with *tulle*, &c.; and, although it is not very courtier-like to say so, we may add that the lady in question was remarkably stout, and of the middle age;—

"That on her cheek, and eke her nose,

In great abundance bloom'd the rose."

She might, in fact, be compared to the arbutus loaded with scarlet fruit, mentioned by the poet Ovid [15]—a description which ought to be very gratifying, for does not the proverb tell us that "a blush is the complexion of virtue?" The queen wore a profusion of beautiful blue-black hair, and the expression of her countenance indicated that it was possible for her, now and then, to entertain strong opinions of her own. She was, in fact, or rather is, what vulgar people would call "a lusty woman."

The opera-house is internally pretty, and very French in appearance. The presence of so many bright uniforms, profusely adorned with various orders of knighthood, contributed much to the brilliancy of the scene. Of the performance we have little or nothing to say. The same old operas which are in vogue on the fashionable stage of other European capitals are repeated here, and no new flight is attempted. Here also a curious operatic problem, which we had previously endeavoured to solve at London and Paris, suggested itself to us, wherefore, namely, a married man or father on the stage should invariably have a bass voice, a villain a baritone, and a lover or *batelier* a tenor? I am not aware that in ordinary life, when we enter the holy state of matrimony, our voices as a rule descend from tenor to bass, or that gentlemen who have to leave England on *urgent business* for a few years, come back with their tones perceptibly deepened. No doubt, however, such profound students of real life as operatic managers must have a good reason for all they do.

FOOTNOTES:

[13] Within the Escorial everything is on a colossal scale. There are 16 courts, 40 altars, 1,111 windows outside, and 1,562 inside. There are 12,000 doors, 86 staircases, and 15 sets of cloisters. There are galleries of 300 feet in length, painted in elaborate fresco, 89 fountains; and if one traversed the entire fabric in all its parts, one would have to walk ninety and odd miles. It is considered by the Spaniards as the eighth wonder of the world.

[14] Shirley.

[15] "Pomo onerata rubenti arbutus."

CHAPTER IX.

A BULL-FIGHT.—THE ARENA.—THE SPECTATORS.—PROCESSION.—THE BULL.—APPEARANCE OF THE MEN AND HORSES.—NIMBLE FOOTMEN.—THE COMBAT.—SCENE OF HORROR.—THE BANDERILLEROS.—THE ESPADA.—DEATH OF THE BULL.

I, of course, paid a visit to that peculiarly Spanish institution, the circus, in which the people of Madrid are accustomed to glut their savage taste for blood. Immense crowds were bending their footsteps in the direction of the great national spectacle, and like a straw in a torrent I was carried with them along the glaring and dusty road. The roar of the multitude was deafening, and shouts of laughter pealed in the air. The people were arrayed in their gayest holiday attire of lace and gold; and the young women flashed their bright eyes and tossed their black hair in response to the sallies of their cavaliers. Proud dames were borne through the rushing stream in stately carriages, attended by handsome gallants, pushing forward their foaming horses to keep by the side of the fair ones whose favour they sought. High and low, rich and poor, the young maiden and the gallant youth, the strong soldier and the tottering beggar, troops of children and aged crones,—an entire city's people—were jostling each other to be forward in the throng among the thousand horses and vehicles of every sort, and the masses of those who were on foot hastening in the blinding dust and heat along that yellow road.

The building in which the favourite sport takes place is an amphitheatre, having some resemblance to that of old Rome, open at the roof, through which a circle of the soft heavens can be seen hanging above like a broad and azure banner. An eager and seething multitude were struggling and pushing for entrance through the numerous doors and passages, until bank after bank was dark with the thick crowds of men, and all the balconies glowed with the bright garments, waving fans, and fair faces of women. Below was an extensive round space of ground, on which sand and sawdust were spread in anticipation of the approaching slaughter. It is difficult to convey the impression with which I heard around me in such a place the laughter of young girls and the prattle of little children. I could not but wonder for what reason these young creatures had been brought thither. When, at last, the seats and benches of the whole wide circle were filled, the walls seemed white with twelve thousand faces, and glowed with endless colours, while myriads of fans were constantly waving, and the hum of impatience proceeded from the vast assemblage.

At length a trumpet sounded with a loud, clear tone; a sigh of relief arose from the expectant multitude; and their eyes flashed with joy as the sun poured down upon the great ring of sand below in rays of dazzling light. The doors of the arena were opened wide, and a gay procession, consisting of those who were to take part in the sport, made its entrance, accompanied by the sound of martial music. A cavalcade of lancemen [16] and horsemen, clad in the velvet gear of a bygone age, were most conspicuous. [17] These were preceded by a band of footmen, decked in brave array of gold lace, their garments of the brightest hues, orange, violet, rose, and crimson. These men had over their shoulders numerous red cloths and scarlet flags, besides which each one carried in his hand a naked sword. The procession was closed by teams of mules, gaily attired, dragging at their heels a great iron hook.

This gallant company was a pleasant enough sight to the eye; and the maiden's cheek might well redden as the graceful forms of the strong young men, with thew and sinew swelling round and fair beneath the tight jackets of satin, the coloured pantaloons, and the silken hose, passed erect below, glittering bravely in the sunlight that streamed upon them. They all made a low salute to him who was master of the sports that day, and immediately after the arena was cleared of all save three lancemen, sitting silent and still on the backs of lean horses, which had their eyes closely bandaged. The various footmen, each with red cloak in hand, lingered around, behind, or nigh to the high wooden barriers surrounding the ring, as if in case of some anticipated danger.

When the hour announced for the commencement of the sport arrived, the vast assemblage became hushed in silence, which was at last broken by a shrill trumpet-peal that suddenly pierced the air. After a moment of suspense, a broad wooden door flew open, and in rushed a wild bull of Andalusia, decked with a flowing riband, or moña. The formidable-looking animal halted in mid-career, and with loud ominous snorts, glared savagely around at the great array of its persecutors, at the same time pawing the ground with ire, and wildly lashing its angry tail. In another instant, with his long horns lowered and levelled, and amidst a cloud of dust, he dashed round the ring swift as a bolt discharged from a catapult, hurling into the air, or casting down on the earth, everything in his path. Three horses which were in his way fell headlong with their riders in confused and dusty heaps, and lay quivering on the ground. The poor animals were disembowelled, and their blood tinged the sand, a sight which was greeted with the cry of "Bravo, Toro!" ringing from twelve thousand throats. A score of footmen leapt down into the ring, and quickly scoured to the scene of action, waving their scarlet mantles in the eyes of the enraged bull to draw off its attention from the *picadores*, who lay prostrate beneath their wounded horses. At the same time the mules were driven in, and the hook being applied, they galloped off with the carrion, which left a broad red track behind it. The bull, meanwhile, charging here, charging there, dashed now after one foe, now after another, as they darted about, carefully avoiding the long horns, which missed their mark, perhaps only by an inch, as the runner, stopping suddenly, leapt nimbly on one side, and left the furious beast to turn in pursuit of fresh tormentors, trailing a flaunting banner before his eyes. In one of his furious charges he came against the wooden barrier of the arena with a crash that shook the building. He was only half a foot behind the lithe form of one of his enemies, who assured his safety by vaulting over the barrier. A moment or two later, or an orange peel in his path, and no human power could have saved him.

After a series of impetuous charges, the first strength of the bull being exhausted, he was left panting for a short time without provocation, until the gates admitted three fresh lancemen, who urged their sorry blindfolded hacks into the ring with the sharp angles of their ample Moorish stirrups. With a wild snort, a shower of foam falling from his mouth, the bull rushed at the nearest horse; but the dexterous horseman, receiving the charge obliquely with the point of his lance, although well-nigh dismounted by the shock, caused the great beast to rear aside with the sudden smart. A shout of "Bravo, Picador!" arose from the crowd; but ere it ceased, the baffled brute, directing its attack against another opponent, had buried its horns up to its forehead in the ribs of the nearest horse, which, blinded as it was, stood there a mere butt for the onset. The rider's lance at the same moment was plunged into the neck of the bull, and blood flowed in torrents.

A fierce light now glared in the eyes of the people, of man and of maiden, as if the most ferocious instincts had been awakened in them. Near me I saw, in their private balcony, a stately dame alone with her beautiful daughter, both gazing with the deepest interest on the bloody contest. Some young ladies, the daughters of haughty grandees, were actually listening in such a place to the whispers of love from gallant young nobles, while they reclined luxuriously among cushions and flowers. Men were even beating with iron rods the fetlock joints of the dying horses, lest they should fail ere the bull was spent. Ripped and mangled as they were, they were compelled to stand on their legs for another onslaught. I can never forget one poor horse which I saw trotting across the ring to meet each charge with his entrails dragging in the dust. Another wretched animal, from whose eyes the bandage had fallen, looked around on the vast assemblage with an appealing glance; but there was no mercy in any heart that beat there.

Again a trumpet sounded, and several young men appeared in gay attire of lace, silk, and embroidery, with the velvet bonnet of Spain on their crisp shaved heads. The agility of their supple limbs seemed to equal that of the antelope; their forms were graceful as that of Apollo, and they were fearless as young lions. These, the *banderilleros*, bore in either hand long iron arrows, keen and barbed, to each of which was attached a web of coloured ribbons.

The powerful beast—though rage still burned in his lurid eyes, and foam fell from his dilated nostrils and quivering flank—now showed signs of languor, and a more uncertain though still threatening front. One of the *banderilleros* advanced boldly in front of the bull, in dangerous proximity to his sharp, bloody horns. He waved his arms, and brandished his ribboned darts as if he were derisively taunting the rabid beast. It seemed dangerous to presume thus much, for the bull, excited to madness, suddenly rushed on him; but cool and watchful, the man lightly stepped aside as if disdaining to move one superfluous inch. As the animal passed him in his furious career, the darts with their ribbons were buried with the speed of lightning in his gory neck. With a wild bellow of rage and pain the furious brute makes at another foe in his path, but distracted by the number of his persecutors dancing like demons around him, and exhausted by the loss of blood, he sinks fainting to the earth, though still to the last defiant, amongst the yells of the excited crowd.

In a few minutes a man with a bright, naked sword, called the *espada*, entered the arena, and demanded permission from the *autoridad* to kill the bull. This was accorded amid the increasing buzz and restlessness of the crowd. Carrying in his left hand a dark red flag, to act as a bait for the still sensitive eye of the *toro*, and in his right a good Toledan blade, the *espada* cautiously advanced towards the crouching beast, more dangerous now, perhaps, than in the full vigour of his strength. The man appeared to be the incarnation of address as opposed to brute-force; firm of nerve, sharp of sight, undaunted in courage. Approaching to within eight inches of his glaring foe, he stood face to face with him, prepared for mortal struggle. Waving the red flag to the left, to lure away the horns from the front of his chest, he slowly raised his long sword up to the level of his eye, and then drew back his arm with as little motion as possible, to make the fatal plunge at that narrow point in the neck where the spinal cord may best be severed, that immediate death may ensue. As the blow was delivered, the beast, swerving aside, dashed at the red flag waving in his face, his long horns almost grazing the man's left breast, while the steel was plunged to the hilt into his body. The blow had not been fairly struck, and the mad brute darted away, carrying with him the *espada's* sword, the blood spouting in jets at every stride. A shout of execration proceeded from all the balconies at this unlucky blow, which should have laid the bull motionless. The bull-fighter, meanwhile, determined to retrieve his reputation, remained calm as at first. Crying with a loud voice to some functionary for *el cachete*, he received a small, sharp dagger, which he screwed slowly and carefully round within the hollow of his right hand. Arranging once more the dark red flag in his left, he calmly awaited the onslaught of the bull. The great brute, still formidable, made straight to the middle of the ring, where his opponent stood, and when his eye caught again the hated red flag which the *espada* was waving in his face, he pulled up short, with concentrated rage and fury.

As the two thus stood face to face,—the desperate beast and the single man with his bodkin,—we were reminded of Glaucus of Pompeii fronting the lion with his *stylus*, while the crowd of the amphitheatre thirsted for his blood. The bull-fighter kept his eye fixed on that of the bull, which had it not been for a slow oscillation of the head—as his eyes seemed to follow, fascinated, the gentle waving of the flag—would have appeared motionless. The man crept to within an inch of the long horn-points, cautiously and slowly extending his right arm with the dagger over the animal's neck, and stretching his body forward till the left horn almost touched his chest. The eye of the bull was still distracted by the red flag which was incessantly waved before him, amidst the most profound silence. Suddenly, like a flash of light, the knife was brought down, the exact point was hit, and the ponderous brute rolled over, weltering in a dark torrent of gore. Showers of flowers were thrown on the victor's head by fair hands above, who thus testified that in their eyes the brave man had retrieved his fault. The gaudy mules once more dashed in, and in a moment galloped back again, dragging the great carcass behind them.

How impressive are the contrasts of nature! At the moment when this scene of blood was brought to an end, a lark soared calmly across the blue circle of the quiet heavens above, while near to me a fair young mother hushed her new-born infant to sleep.

FOOTNOTES:

[16] Picadores.

[17] Police of the ring, who preserve from custom their mediæval costume, and are a mere form.

CHAPTER X.

TOLEDO.—VIEW OF THE CITY.—THE CATHEDRAL.—PROCESS OF SMOKE-DRYING.—ALMANZA.—VALENCIA.—THE FONDA DE MADRID.—A BENEVOLENT DOCTOR.—SPANISH MULETEERS.—HOW CONTROVERSIES ARE SETTLED.

OH! Toledo, imperial city, beloved of the old Goth, rich home of the Moor and Jew, [18] and chosen throne of the Emperor of the West, [19] how art thou fallen! And yet thy destiny has only been that which awaits all cities, all nations. Still the old town has a proud and lofty aspect on its rock-built seat, and though the splendours for which it was once celebrated are now mouldering, it still looks down with haughty glance on the feeble kingdom beneath, and its insolent modern capital in the midst. A volume might well be devoted to the description of Toledo, which is still magnificent even in ruins, and inexhaustible in objects of interest; but as we mean to explore some of the regions and cities of the warmer South, and even to extend our journey to the Spanish islands of the Mediterranean, we may not indulge in more than a passing glance at the crumbling walls, the falling palaces, and the Oriental courts of the old metropolis of Spain.

A view of the city from any advantageous position in its neighbourhood is very imposing. The venerable hue of antiquity is upon the whole place; and there is not a street in which there are not buildings that have been connected with important events in the history of Spain. As seen from a distance, its sombre towers rising from the treeless Vega [20] have a striking resemblance to a great fretted crown, such as might have been worn by some old barbarian giant, while the green fields through which the Tagus pursues its course appear like a green velvet cushion on which the royal diadem reposes. As we approached nearer we could judge more accurately of the height of the majestic rock on which the town, like a great castle, is built. The streets are generally steep and winding. Those of Moorish origin are very narrow, and it is difficult to find one's way through them. Their narrowness has this advantage, that it affords a protecting shadow from the oppressive heat of the noonday sun. Some of the churches are splendid specimens of Gothic architecture, though, from being towerless, they are occasionally heavy in aspect. There are many fine examples of the Mediæval and Saracenic styles, the graceful, airy-like character of the latter having something peculiarly attractive in it. But the interest of all we see attaches only to the past; the life of the city has departed long ago; and we walk through its silent streets as in a dream.

The cathedral—one of the richest in the world—is of very ancient origin; its foundation belonging to a period far back in the history of Spain. Many are the changes which it has undergone in the revolutions of the Peninsula. When the Moors conquered the city it was turned into a mosque; when in 1085 Alphonzo V. recovered Toledo, it remained, according to the king's promise, still devoted to the religious service of the Moslem, until the Archbishop of Toledo in the following year summarily destroyed all the insignia of Saracenic worship within it, and it became again a temple of the Catholic faith. A century passed, and St. Ferdinand levelled the edifice, which he felt was tainted with an unclean spirit, to the ground. A new building was then conceived on a magnificent plan; and after two hundred years' incessant labour the present splendid edifice was completed.

The general effect of its exterior, though marred by the close proximity of surrounding buildings, is exceedingly striking. Like a magnificent jewel showing its great lustre at every turn of its cutting, there is no point of view from which it cannot be seen to advantage. The cupola is a work of great taste, and the open work of the Muzarabic chapel is remarkably elegant. The stately portals, worthy of the fane to which they give admission, are of the most elaborate Gothic, and the grand *façade*, rich with ornament, is a work of inexhaustible detail and wonderful finish. The open work of the parapet is no less admirable. The three stories of the *façade* may be said to be densely peopled with magnificent statues, and the solitary belfry tower, from which ascends an elegant spire, rising to the height of 330 feet above the gloomy and silent old streets below, is crowned by a vast tiara encircling with its iron rays the great cross surmounting the whole.

The interior of the cathedral is in every way worthy of the noble aspect of the exterior. If even the idle stranger is struck with sentiments of veneration when he surveys its noble proportions—its lofty vaulted roof and its long aisles—what must be the feeling of the worshipper who comes inspired by faith to pray in such a temple?

The coloured windows are works of high art, in perfect harmony with the spirit and design of this noble cathedral. While we were examining them, the organ suddenly pealed out its solemn tones, and we knew not which most to admire—the thunder-like roll which at one moment filled the building, or the silvery sweetness of the notes by which it was followed. *Sic transit gloria mundi*; and truly, in such a place as old Toledo, or in the older sepulchres of the past, in Rome or Thebes, the heart of the passing pilgrim feels the weight of ages heavy upon it. Life seems to move with a slower pace, and the reflective mind is carried back to the dim eras of remotest history.

I like old cities; for there is no panorama of such grandeur as that suggested by the sight of their ruins, when the mind can call up as in a series of stately pictures those great events which have left their stamp on all ages. And no country has a history richer than that of Spain in grand and stirring incidents, or a more ample store of those venerated memorials which tell the Spaniards of the present day what their ancestors were.

How delicious it was, at night, to linger at the open casement of the quaint old Toledan *fonda*, and look down upon the quiet streets of the ancient city, watching the few passengers in them, while the moon shed its silvery rays on the dark old buildings, and over the far plains beyond. It was a beautiful autumn evening, and there came to us, borne along on the soft air, a strain of distant music, wild, strange, and melancholy, like the wailings of some forgotten dirge. It was a fit requiem after the toils of the day, and with the strain in our ears we went to bed and slept.

Now for Valencia and the blue Mediterranean, 306 miles distant. We start an hour before sunset on our sixteen hours' journey. The whistle screams, the train begins to move, everybody lights cigarettes. The windows are all carefully pulled up, and away we glide, wondering how long would be the process of drying, smoking, and curing the human frame into the condition of a preserved Finnan haddock or bloater. Such an atmosphere as that in which we were compelled to breathe sixteen hours, we thought, ought to do it.

Immediately after we left Madrid, our old friends, those dear, flat, uninteresting sandy plains with a few solitary olive-trees here and there, again appeared. By the way, apropos of olives, we may here utter a warning for travellers in this country. There are no half-and-half measures with Spanish olives. They are charming, no doubt, to those who are habitual eaters of them; but to such as are not, we can only say, "God help them!"

We attempted, spite of the smoke, to enjoy a few hours' sleep during the night, and were only awakened from a deep slumber on arriving in the early morning at Almanza, a miserable place with a French *buffet*, a Moorish castle, an historic reputation, and, thank goodness, some fresh air. We got out and walked on the platform, still rather hazy from our troubled slumbers, and found ourselves in the midst of a crowd of eccentric-looking *rusticos* dressed in breeches, jackets, carpets, rags, and velvet hats. We approached a magnificent French gentleman at the buffet, and received a cup of Spanish chocolate. By way of civility we asked him, "What was the difference between the *Chocolat Menier* and the chocolate they gave us here?" We received this answer, "None whatever, monsieur, excepting that ours is much dearer."

Leaving this very recommendatory gentleman, we turned to study the objects of local interest. Here, we thought, as well as everywhere else in Spain, there must be some interesting antiquity, something to remind us of the great men and mighty deeds of the past; and being of an inquiring mind we soon discovered that it was near Almanza that the army of Philip V., commanded by Berwick, gained a victory over the troops of the Archduke of Austria in 1707.

We had made considerable progress, and were now about seventy miles from our journey's end,

With the morning upon us so fresh and fair,

While a breeze sings soft through the ambient air,

People wonder to find it there,—

In a place so hot as Almanza.

About twenty miles beyond that place, as well as we could judge in our rapid course, the vegetation began to improve, and the olives appeared to have a fresher hue, a more vigorous growth. The country, too, became more picturesque, diversified as it was occasionally by rocky hills. We passed, also, what appeared to be deserted villages. For a time, however, this part of the country could not be seen to great advantage, as we had frequently to pass through dark tunnels and deep cuttings. Here and there was an attempt at a vineyard or two, in which the stunted shrubs seemed to grow with great difficulty among the stones and sand. One village which we remarked, pitched on a mountain slope, seemed to be the very place for a band of bandits. The gaps of savage highlands were backed in the distance by purple lines of remote scenery, pencilled, as it seemed, along the sky. The nakedness of the hills was concealed by the pine trees with which their slopes were covered.

The next place we reached was the old brown, tumble-down town of Mogente, basking in a sunlit valley, where grow Indian corn and the prickly pear. Low, whitewashed, terraced *cortijos*, or farm-houses, are scattered upon the rocky slopes, while high over the vale topple some broken towers of the ancient Moor. Onwards we went, across ravines, dry watercourses, and long, straight, white roads, bordered by stone-pines, the olive, and the mulberry. Country people of an Arab-looking aspect, brown, red-sashed, and semi-nude, were jogging along in the sun and dust on sturdy, gaily-dressed mules. Bold peaks, topped with ruined castles, frequently appeared suspended above us as we moved onwards at a rapid rate. The abundant vegetation afforded evidence that we were now in the midst of a more luxuriant soil; while from across the wide garden-like plains, distinguished by that long dark line of sapphire in the distance, the breath of the Mediterranean at length fell soothingly upon the brow.

As we drew towards our journey's end we passed several more towns, but so rapidly that they seemed like the phantoms of a dream. We could descry, however, their rich churches and spiring *campanarios* nestling amongst deep green bowers. At one point of our progress we observed a long Moorish wall, with its ancient battlements, scaling in yellow zig-zags the steep mountain's side, till it joined a fortress on the summit. White tombs, shaded by mournful cypress, sometimes reminded us of Eastern lands. In all directions the stately palm-tree waves aloft its graceful plumage, and the orange first greets the eye, while lonely convents are seen perched like eagles' eyries high on rocky summits, looking down upon a paradise of brilliant green, and fruits of gold, spread in the fertile vale below. The glowing plains, and the waving lines of the light grey hills, are all lit up by sparkling villages, silver streamlets, and the rays of the glorious sun. Onwards we speed through groves of the feathering palm, with their grape-like clusters of yellow dates, through bowers of deep green foliage, and through corn and rice-fields. We dash rapidly through high walled Moorish towns, with the palm-trees rising in their warm streets, in which are reposing from their toil Bedouin-like figures; and over patches of stony waste land, sown with great aloes and the Indian fig. On one side are thick plantations of bamboo and cane, and on the other gardens of lemons, melons, and rosy pomegranate. In fact, the approach to Valencia, the Sultana of Spanish cities, is in Europe, perhaps, well-nigh unrivalled. The curtain rises, as we have seen, upon stony wastes and desert plains, and falls upon all that tropical vegetation which is peculiar to the beauteous climate and rich soil of Eastern Spain. This is the busiest part of the country; and besides the orange, lemon, palm, cactus, and pomegranate, we find rice, flax, corn, pepper, and tobacco growing in wild luxuriance, until the white gates of Valencia open to receive us.

On descending from the train, near the beautiful classic circle of the *Plaza de los Toros*, we jumped into a *Tartana* [21]—a wonderful black vehicle, hooded over, like a gondola on wheels, or a cart in which they carry away the dead in time of plague—and on we rattled, trying very hard to look as if we enjoyed the peculiar sensation produced by the absence of springs. The pavement resembled nothing on earth, unless it were the roadway of Regent Street as it might appear strewn with stones from a druidical circle. It was perfectly useless attempting to smoke, for the cigarette was just as likely to enter the eye or the ear as the mouth. Thus we jolted and bumped on through cool lofty streets, so narrow that the rays of the sun, save for one hour of the day, can never visit their depths. Here we were again in a thoroughly Spanish town. The houses were painted in brilliant colours, pink, blue, green, and red, and there were numerous balconies, from which blinds, and mats, and carpets, of every hue, were drooping.

On we jolted, swinging round sharp angles, bringing quaint old houses of ancient grandees into sudden view before us, and ever and anon coming upon noble churches, sculptured over with wondrous devices up to the topmost towers, that reeled with the clang of bells. Again we dived sharply into a labyrinth of dark narrow alleys, swarming with busy crowds, with all the goods and wares half out into the street, and filling the dilapidated balconies—a scene of life and bustle which nothing can rival, save the bazaars of Smyrna or Stamboul. With a fearful bump we swung round a church corner in the bright, gay, open sunlight into squares whose spacious mansions look down upon gardens of palms, trumpet-flowers, aloes, acacias, and oleanders, all watered by the spray from marble fountains, springing up high in the midst. In a few minutes, however, we were down again into a narrow, picturesque, and dirty *calle*, filled with priests with shovel-hats, Murillo-like urchins, all rags and grins, gaudy mules, and men dressed in breeches, sash, and broad velvet *sombreros*, with long coloured *mantas* thrown gracefully across their shoulders; while, high above, the opposite eaves of the dark wooden houses nearly meet, exhibiting between them only a long band of deep blue sky.

Rattling on, we burst once more into a wide, busy market-place, with town-hall, tower, and church, all elaborately sculptured, and with low, dark arcades burrowing beneath the houses. The open space was gay with the coloured awnings of merchants' stalls, and alive with buyers and sellers. The hum of many voices and the cries of water-carriers were heard all around us. In a word, the market-scene from Masaniello was before us. Here were piles of magnificent fruit and vegetables from the fertile *campana* around the city; there vast heaps of oranges and melons, with great bunches of yellow dates and purple grapes, were heaped upon the ground. Fish from the near Mediterranean were exposed for sale, and assortments of large earthen vases, made in the neighbourhood, were still hardening in the sun. We saw on all sides groups of stately long-eyed women, glancing out from beneath the shade of the mantilla, with classic features and luxuriant blue-black hair; others, robed in dresses of fantastic dye, pressing naked brown infants to the breast as they talked and sold at their stalls. Whole caravans, drawn by large mules dressed in trappings, and tinkling with bells, stalked past us; and strong oxen, yoked together by the head, drawing heavily-laden carts by the sheer force of their necks and horns alone, made their way slowly over the place, while some semi-wild dogs snatched at their heels as they were disturbed during their bask in the sun. There was the trim, upright *torero* [22] with shaved lip and short crisp whiskers, dressed in his every-day suit of braided jacket, red sash, tight trouser, pigtail, and velvet hat, while the swinging forms of the mountaineer in his goat-skin, and of the stalwart peasant, with his coloured *manta* sweeping from his shoulder, and his feet in sandals, passed through the midst. The everlasting *cigarillo* was smoking from their lips, and the gaudy kerchief hung down upon their necks from beneath the black velvet bonnet.

Beautiful fountains grace the streets, and rows of acacias wave like feathers in the breeze. Nothing, in fact, can be conceived more picturesque than the narrow streets, with church and palace, with coloured houses, with balconies and banner-like awnings; nothing more calm than the climate, nothing more brilliant than the ever-changing scenes in the *plazas*, nothing more interesting than the motley cigarette-smoking crowds, so different from the dingy mob of a London street; finally, nothing more Spanish than the entire picture.

We landed at the *Fonda de Madrid*, where we intended to take up our quarters; but before ascending the spacious marble stairs we found it necessary to make way for a troop of blind beggars who were being conducted down step by step by their friends. These poor creatures were suffering from the local disease of ophthalmia, and the cause of their assemblage on the present occasion was, that once a week a good doctor holds a levee in the hotel for the gratuitous treatment of their malady, *para caridad y para el amor de Dios*. Such disinterested benevolence, which is by no means uncommon among medical men in all countries, is very praiseworthy; but at the same time we are bound to confess that the sights which are sometimes brought under our eyes on such occasions are far from agreeable to casual tourists.

The train by which we had arrived was—considering that it was one of the *cosas de España*—naturally late. We had been altogether eighteen hours on the journey from Madrid. However, before breaking our fast, in fact immediately on our arrival at the *fonda* at Valencia, we naturally asked for the sea. "Three miles off at the port of El Grao," [23] was the answer. Here, *acqui, tout de suite, una tartana*, look sharp! and we were immediately rushing through the streets, and out of the city into the long yellow roads, with the sand and dust up to the axle of the two-wheeled gondola, in quest of our bath. We passed over a splendid bridge, spanning the waterless river Turia or Guadalaviar, and commanding a splendid view of Valencia, with all its coloured spires and domes resting against the spotless sky. We were driven through a long avenue of acacias and palms until, as we were going due east, we were naturally brought up by the sea. "A boat, a boat,"—*batel, batel!* we exclaimed; and in answer to our summons, about twenty almost naked fishermen with red rags round their loins immediately pulled to shore, like a swarm of minnows attracted by a piece of bread; but although we wanted a *batel*, we had no desire to fight. However, in a few minutes we were stripped and swimming away merrily on the buoyant wave, so deep, clear, and blue; inhaling health, strength, and delight at every stroke. The rugged outlines of the lofty mountains of the Spanish coast were gradually fading from sight in the morning haze, while, afar off, as we lay motionless on our backs floating on the calm surface of the sea, the eye caught the distant gleam of the long sail of many a felucca, softly pink in the reflection of the morning's glow.

Ah! those careless days, snatched from the serious toil of our existence, they come not again. Those sunny holidays which we enjoyed in the society of friendship, how happy, though few, they were, and how delightful it is to recall them to memory! They come but rarely, and at distant intervals, but for that reason they are only the more delightful. They pass quickly, but their memory is as green as ever, and in calling to mind our various wanderings, we feel almost as delighted as we actually did when our footsteps ranged at freedom in a strange land and under a foreign sky. Well may the desponding poet sing:—

"Count o'er the joys thy life hath seen,

Count o'er the days from anguish free,

And know whatever thou hast been,

'Tis something better—not to be."

Back again then we turned, through the acacias, the palms, the glare and the dust, and over the old bridge with its statues, spanning the waterless river. We passed the grim old fortress-gates of other days, and walls topped with mouldering battlements, standing up before the nineteenth century to verify the former strength of the Moorish conqueror. We again went through the perfumed gardens and wide white *plazas*, all glowing in the sun; the dim labyrinthine streets once more received us; and, stumbling out from the black plague-cart, we were soon within the beggar-haunted *fonda*. Here we discussed a meal, consisting of enormous prawns, like reptiles swimming in oil, and of red chocolate, sweetened with mare's milk and cinnamon. But as the proverb says, "the jaw of man brought all evil into the world," we suppose, therefore, it is meet that it should suffer occasional retribution; and sure enough it *will* suffer it among some of those *cosas de España* which have no resemblance to those of any other country.

To turn out into the streets of a foreign town—the more foreign the better—is a great delight; to go forth alone and see where fate will lead us, and to wander and meditate, undisturbed by cackling guide, who, with the spirit of plagiarism which is characteristic of his race, waits until we have informed him of some historic fact, and then tells it back again in half-an-hour as his own information. Follow us then, gentle reader, and bear with the eccentric "order of our going," and in your amiability, favour us by remembering that that which may seem disorder to some is with others a law of their nature which they must obey. So we pray

"Whoe'er thou art that read'st this errant book,

Slight it not for its method, so as to

Reject it; but into it we pray thee look;

It may meet with thine heart before thou go." [24]

Out again into the hot, bright squares, and then into the old Gothic cathedral, where we found ourselves in comparative darkness, in the enjoyment of a very agreeable coolness. This ancient ecclesiastical structure is built on the remains of a Moorish mosque which had itself arisen from the ruins of Roman temples. How agreeable was the contrast between the hot, garish day without, and the dim, religious light of the old church, with its mysterious incense-laden atmosphere, gemmed with a hundred twinkling lights, and traversed by brilliant rays from the coloured windows, rays which fell in various hues upon the marble statues standing ghost-like against the venerable walls, and lighting up the lofty spears of brazen screening until they seemed like fiery arrows shot up from the world beneath by some unmeasured bow. Such was the spirit of the place, that I felt as if I could have joined in the devotion of the shrouded figures who were kneeling silent and still upon the marble pavement, while every thought seemed to rise heavenward with the noble strains of the organ. We emerged again into the heat and blaze of the crowded streets, through which troops of dusty soldiery were threading their way, and in which the blare of martial music was mingled with the clash of the church's bells. We found our way into a stately market-place, in the midst of the bustle of which we got entangled in a procession of the Virgin. As it was quite a characteristic scene, we thought it worth looking at, even though the delay cost us a few moments. A little boy in scarlet drawers and embroidered shirt led the way, making a hideous noise on a drum. He was followed by four seedy-looking gentlemen with vacant faces, and without hats, dressed in respectable every-day suits of black, bearing long, lighted candles. Next, making unnatural strides, and tricked out in muslin and tinfoil,—like "My Lady" of the sweeps on the first of May,—came two unfortunate little girls of about twelve years of age, carrying trays of rose-leaves. These poor children, from this unwonted exercise, seemed very puffy and red in the face. Then came the *pièce de résistance* of the entertainment. Four ragged peasants in goat's skin and sandals bore along on their shoulders a palanquin, or rather a piece of an old wooden door, which supported a great wax doll, whose cheeks were of the deepest vermilion, with a tin hat or crown on its head, and a piece of ordinary Manchester coloured cotton kerchief tied by a string round its waist. The procession was closed by several men bearing flags, and by a band of music, the members of which, in the uniform of old soldiers, produced with their instruments music so original in its character that I am unable to give the reader any conception of it. The band, as usual everywhere else, was surrounded and followed by a large crowd of idlers, of chattering old women, dark-eyed maidens, and yelling urchins, who, notwithstanding their appreciation of the strains which they heard, lost no opportunity of performing various practical jokes upon the public generally. Knots of men, with skins burnt to the darkest brown hue, and clad in striped mantles, velvet sombreros, and sashes, with their legs bandaged, and their feet in apostolic-looking sandals, were sauntering in the street, followed by some stray dogs and a loose mule or two. Anything like the noise they all made as they threaded their passage through the crowd, cannot be conceived. Their incessant chattering somewhat resembled that heard in the parrot-house of our Zoological Gardens.

In the province of Valencia, if we may believe their statistical authorities, there is an average of six hundred murders per annum. And the judicial mind of the Valencians is very amenable to lenity towards the accused, under the softening influence of Spanish money equal in amount to about three pounds sterling. The value of human life does not appear to be estimated very highly by the masses, and it is frequently sacrificed on very slight occasions. A few words at a tavern, a little heat in argument, or a slight difference of opinion, will generally end in one of the disputants finding six inches of cold steel entering his vitals in some unsuspecting moment. A sharp knife is found to be a very decisive method of settling all controversies, whatever may be their nature. These knives, which are sold in the shops avowedly for the purpose for which they are used, are very formidable instruments, with blades from three inches to a foot and a half in length, and with this inscription engraved thereon, "Soi sola para defender el onor." However, after our own Todmorton heroes, and young gentlemen who pass their time in pursuit of science by dissecting little children in woods and carrying about their eyes in their pockets, we cannot well blame the Spaniards for endeavouring, in the indulgence of such little social amenities, to keep up in the race with other civilised nations.

FOOTNOTES:

[18] Called Toledoth by the Jew, who shared its riches with the Moor.

[19] Charles V.

[20] The Vega, now a desert, was once a perfect forest of palms and mulberry trees.

[21] Derived possibly from the Russian "Tarantass," or springless carriage.

[22] Bull-fighter.

[23] El Grao. Grado, grades,—steps to the sea.

[24] Bunyan.

CHAPTER XI.

VOYAGE TO THE BALEARES.—MAJORCA.—PALMA DE MALLORCA.—OUR APPREHENSION.—FONDA DE LAS TRES PALOMAS.—HISTORICAL NOTICES.—DON JAYME.—THE RAMBLA.—COSTUME.—LANGUAGE.—CLIMATE.— CHARACTER OF THE PEOPLE.

ALLONS donc, en route for the Balearic Isles, or the Baleares, the birth-place of the great Hannibal, and for Palma, the capital, situated in the south-western portion of the island of Majorca.

"Minora canamus," says the Latin poet.

"Majorca canamus," say we.

"Ibiça, Majorca, and Minorca are islands belonging to Spain, lying to the east of that country, in the Mediterranean. From them the ancient Romans enlisted into their armies the famous Balearic slingers, who were compelled to strike their meals from the roofs of their houses before they were allowed to eat them." This is what everyone learns by rote at school, and after he leaves it—when the pupil is supposed to have finished his education, a thing at once very easy and very difficult to accomplish,—the islands are never mentioned or dreamt of again during life.

Behold us, then, starting for this *terra incognita* of Majorca, [25] that remote and unfortunate region to which Mr. Murray has never wandered, and of which Bradshaw has never sung. In fact, before sailing we almost began to doubt the propriety of venturing to a place so far beyond the bounds of civilisation as to be beneath the notice of these gentlemen. Although our fears scarcely went so far as to imagine that these islands were among those localities, of which we had read so much in our youth, inhabited by dancing savages with plumes of feathers in their heads, stuck all over with scalping knives and tomahawks, and who prefer human blood to any other beverage, still we did not know to what inconveniences, to what hard-ships, we might be exposed in a place to which we had never heard the slightest allusion made by any one, probably because nothing good could be said of it. However, we were in for it, *Prêt d'accomplir*, as the Earls of Shrewsbury say, and so we were off for the Balearic capital; and we intend to speak most impartially of Palma, not forgetting the apt, though hackneyed quotation, *Palmam qui meruit ferat*.

The illustrious steam-ship *El Rey Jayme II*, [26] of 150 tons, a vessel reputed tolerably safe, steamed in a truly Spanish and stately manner out of the harbour. The Mediterranean was like a lake, as indeed it is; and as the hours waned, the western sky blushed down in one vast flaming glory upon the long purple line of the Valencian mountains, which rose in lofty majesty along the retiring coast of the Spanish peninsula, now dimly and indistinctly seen. The day fell softly, as all that is most beautiful must fall.

"Soft day, so sweet, so calm, so bright,

The bridal of the earth and sky,

The dew shall weep thy fall to-night

For thou must die."

And so the land vanished from view, and we were alone on the deck on one of those calm and beautiful nights which naturally dispose the mind to meditation. The stars, sparkling like gems of silver on the brow of night, were reflected in the transparent waters of the Mediterranean, where they flashed like jewels in the dark tresses of an Eastern maiden. Lines of phosphoric light marked our course as the prow of the ship cut through the sapphire sea, and were reflected, as it were, in the depths of the heavenly ocean above by the broad opal zone of the milky way, which gleamed with inconceivable lustre.

This is all very fine when the weather is fair and the sea calm; but it is very difficult to be romantic when suffering from sea-sickness, and there was no knowing how painfully prosy we might become ere the two hundred miles of sea, which we had to traverse before we could reach our destination, were passed. At the outset of this little voyage, we could well imagine "the exemplary youth" in the story books asking all sorts of appropriate questions, thus:—

"And so, sir, this is the Mediterranean?" the young Arthur might be supposed to say to his aged tutor.

"Yes, my boy," that learned man might reply, with tears in his eyes at the thought that all his care and solicitude for his pupil should at last be so well repaid by this instance of precocious intelligence, showing that the seed he had sown had borne ample fruit. "Yes, my boy, this indeed is that tideless and lovely sea which has ever presented a problem to the man of science, and a subject for the poet's verse."

But in about four hours after our departure, neither the exemplary youth nor the aged tutor would have been in any very eager mood for edifying question and instructive answer. A howling gale came on, and people, becoming perfectly green in the face, arose one by one from the supper table in a manner they had assumed as remarkably easy and graceful, assuring everybody that they never felt better in their lives, and then disappeared entirely from the vision of their fellow-travellers, and in most cases fellow-sufferers. One old lady, indeed, looked as if she were going to say every moment,—

"I think, captain, as the ship is so very unsteady I would rather get out."

However, some use is generally to be found in everything, and to a person who wishes to stretch a pair of new canvas shoes, that they may be easier on his feet, there is no surer mode than that of walking the deck in a gale of wind.

The sun rose upon us next day in a flood of warm and cloudless glory, and, as his rays chased away the last dark clouds of night in the west, we observed rising before us from the sea, though yet at some distance, the rugged coast of Majorca. Though we could not yet distinguish the wild scenery for which the island is remarkable,—that varied landscape of plain, rock, and gorge,—we could distinctly perceive the noble range of lofty mountains in the centre, invisible at their base, but with their white peaks piercing the high heavens. Steadily the ship cleaved its way through the tranquil sea, until, upon rounding a rocky headland, a distant city, of somewhat Eastern aspect, appeared, the most prominent object being a temple of great dimensions rising in the midst. We could also trace the white line of its stone ramparts; after which our eyes rested with pleasure on terraces of shining houses, and on tapering spires, all glittering in the sun, and reflected in the clear mirror beneath in lines of pointed light. This was Palma de Mallorca, capital of the Spanish province of Las Islas Baleares. Its white houses looked like a brood of white sea-birds sitting on the waters, while away in the distance beyond, cutting soft and clear against the sunny air, were the high jagged mountain range and highlands of Majorca.

As we gradually neared the land, we saw some beautiful villages nestling amidst green plantations, and villas crowning the heights of verdant slopes. On we glided, past the ruined walls of the ancient Roman, where, from tower to tower, great chains were fixed to protect the mouth of the harbour, and past crumbling forts, built by the warlike Moor. A few more turns of the clumsy paddles, and the ship is brought to her moorings in a pretty harbour, in which there appeared to be considerable activity, for it was filled with shipping of various nations. The city rose like an amphitheatre from the shore, and the hills behind it were clothed with an abundant growth of olive-trees.

We landed amongst a motley crowd of semi-Arabic sailors, donkey-boys, and soldiers. Fortunately for us, we had no acquaintance among several affectionate gentlemen waiting for their friends, upon whom they precipitated themselves with the most extravagant marks of affection as soon as they landed, kissing them all over their stubbly faces. We had to undergo, as usual, the process of luggage-searching, though not with the usual result, for we were found to have contravened the laws of the *aduana*. An ordinary Valencian knife, which we had bought to take home as a curiosity, being found in our trunk, we were taken for *contrabandistas*, and being immediately formed into a procession, headed by a man bearing the fatal *corpus delicti*, amidst a chorus of such exclamations as "*Caramba, vamonos, vamonos!*" were placed as prisoners between a couple of blood-thirsty looking *aduaneros*, and led off to the *aduana*, or custom-house. Here we were brought up before a severe-looking official, with, as usual, a cigarette in his mouth, from which the smoke was streaming out in clouds, as well as from his nostrils. This gentleman, whose voice was loud, and his manner quick and jerky, darted out several questions in Mallorquin, the meaning of which we but imperfectly understood. "*Somos Inglés*" suddenly, however, struck us as being a brilliant thing to say, and we said it, our friend at the same time making the rash linguistic attempt to add in Spanish, "*Cuanto hay que pagar. Donde está el consul Inglés?*"

We waited to see what result would follow these experiments. The official, with a severe aspect,—not assumed, for it was natural to him,—took out of his pocket a great knife, and began to pare his nails, after the accomplishment of which task he surveyed them with satisfaction, and turned to some other officials, whom he addressed. They conferred together in a knot in a corner of the room, all talking at once with the most wonderful velocity at the top of their voices. A sign was then made to us by the chief to be silent. At the same time, one of his myrmidons went out, and in half-an-hour returned with an order from the English Consul for our liberation. The same person also brought information from that gentleman which seemed greatly to calm their minds, inasmuch as it assured them that we were not, after all, dangerous conspirators come from England, that hot-bed of revolution, to commence an insurrection, and spread fire, death, and desolation throughout Her Catholic Majesty's provinces. We were then politely allowed to go about our business—a permission of which we immediately availed ourselves.

The first thing we did was to start in search of a *fonda*, with a couple of brown boys in red caps carrying our boxes. After passing along the strong-looking ramparts, and through one or two clean, picturesque streets, in which were some mosque-like buildings turned into barracks, we went under a ruined arch, through which, as in a frame, was seen a beautiful glimpse of distant plains and cloud-capped mountains. We then pulled up at a whitewashed building, which, we were informed, was an establishment entitled *La Fonda de las Tres Palomas*, so named after one of the peculiarities of Palma, and, indeed, of most towns of Oriental descent, viz., the pigeons which are seen everywhere whirling about in the air and walking in the streets, completely tame and unmolested.

The Hotel of the Three Pigeons, although tolerably clean, was lamentably deficient in matters of comfort. The bedrooms were simply whitewashed cells. A narrow bedstead, with a mattress stuffed with the leaves of Indian corn, one chair, and a little slender iron tripod, about three feet high, holding a diminutive basin, constituted the furniture. When the British mania for ablution occasionally overtook us, a pint of brown warm water was brought carefully in a coffee-pot, and poured slowly, as if it were molten gold, into the little basin; while the waiter waited to see what we should do with it, and how apply it for personal use. And well he might; for he seemed to be rather a stranger to the process himself. The saloon and reading-room of the hotel was the kitchen; and there the guests assisted at the cooking of their meals, which, however, was, perhaps, about the best thing they could do, as, upon one occasion, the *chef*, in his anxious desire to please, entirely lost his presence of mind, and was about to boil the woodcocks we had ordered for dinner. Why, at the *fondas* of Majorca, one should find the napkins which ought to be used at dinner placed on the washing-stand for the purposes of ablution, and the towels which should be upon the washing-stand placed on the plates at the dinner-table, will probably remain a mystery, of which it would be vain to seek for any explanation.

We spent a lively night or two in the Hotel of the Three Pigeons, occupying many weary hours in sharp combat with a very active and relentless enemy, the morning finding us covered with the marks of the fray. Any individual of a lethargic temperament, or troubled with slow circulation, to whom such stimulants as the bracing sea air, cold baths, rough towels, &c., are recommended, we should simply advise to pass two or three nights on one of these mattresses. The effect is electrifying, and can only be compared to a sort of intermittent galvanism; and as sleep is not generally found under such conditions, we have no doubt the mattresses in question would in America be called eye-openers, or slumber-worriers. However, when the patient has sufficiently undergone the stimulating process, he may arrest the galvanic action by simply supplying himself with a strong light and a piece of damp soap. He must remain for a few minutes perfectly still, until he perceives that his limbs are assuming a darker hue,—a hue dark with moving multitudes,—when he should apply the soap freely to them, continuing the application until the said soap becomes brown and speckly.

The city of Palma is of considerable dimensions, and contains a population of fifty-two thousand persons. Like all modern towns which rise over the ruins of the past, it is uneven and hilly, a peculiarity which adds much to the general picturesqueness of the street scenery. Built on a slope which rises immediately from the sea, and surrounded by the massive stone ramparts of Philip III., it occupies a strong position. The marks of decay, however, are now everywhere visible. The streets are silent, and the walls of palace and fortress are dropping piece-meal into ruin. Palma was built upon the site of an ancient Roman city of the same name—and its appellation may have been suggested by the palm-trees once abounding there, a few of which still rise gracefully here and there from the terraces and gardens.

Nine hundred years before the Christian era, the Balearic Isles, or Gymnesiæ, were peopled by the Greeks. They then fell into the power of the Carthaginians; and, in due course, beneath the sway of Rome. It was Quintus Cecilius Metellus who, a hundred years before the Christian era, founded the city of Palma; and he was honoured by the title of *Balearicus* for his conquest of the three islands. The fame of the warlike prowess of the hardy islanders had reached the ears of the Roman Consul, and, as a defence against the slings and balistas with which he knew he should have to contend upon landing, Metellus caused his galleys to be *armour-plated* with thick hides and skins, a precaution which saved many of his ships and men from destruction. The flower of the island youth became then absorbed in the Roman armies, and it was mainly to the Balearic slingers that Rome herself owed many a victory.

As time passes on, we find the Moors holding the islands in subjection for a space of four hundred years. On the last day of the year 1229, however, Don Jayme, King of Aragon, having, with his fleet, weathered a fearful storm—an event most trying to the faith of his crusaders, and critical to the future of Majorca—landed with his Christian host, and encamped a few miles from the city. On the morning following, the Holy Sacrament was administered to the Soldiers of the Cross, who, burning with sacred zeal and inspired with the ardour of conquerors, marched with horse and foot upon the foe, led by the young king shouting his battle-cry of "Advance, ye braves! By your arms alone the Lord delivers yon country from the grasp of the Infidel. Forward!" As the Christian army, however, upon nearing the enemy, looked upon their great numbers and formidable position, their hearts seemed to fail. Observing this, the chivalrous Don Jayme rode out alone to an open space between the opposing hosts, and, crying aloud to the Virgin to inspire with courage the hearts of her warriors, he bent the knee in fervent prayer. Filled at once with feelings of shame, admiration, and zeal, the leading ranks rushed on to the breach, with a loud cry of "Sancta Maria!" and, in a few hours, over piles of mingled dead, Moor and

Christian, amongst the smoke of burning houses, and the dust and roar of battle, the Christian banner floated over the city of Palma. So here again we may say,

"Palmam qui meruit ferat."

Looking at the city from the sea, it has a very Oriental appearance. This peculiarity is produced by the flat-roofed houses and bare, yellow walls, with the cactus and prickly pear growing against them, the minaret-like steeples and mosque-like buildings, the light arcades and trellis-work of the dwelling-houses, together with the frequent palm, the long bamboo, and the fig growing in all directions. Nothing can be more agreeable than to lounge in the mellow evening along the broad ramparts, against which the blue waters gently splash, and to gaze upon the high mountain range, seen afar off, with the rocky summits tinged with a pinkish hue by the reflection of the sun's declining rays. This walk is the Rambla, or public promenade, on which, although the dire *chignon* is, we fear, beginning to exhibit its deformity, one may meet with many a lovely daughter of the South draped in the black lace shawl and the graceful mantilla. Amongst the female peasants, a peculiar form of head-dress is adopted, called the Rebosiño, more quaint, we think, than elegant. It consists of a stiff frill radiating from the head and face, while from the nape of the neck depends a single long plait of hair, which is caught in with the sash encircling the waist. In fact, the entire costume is very similar to that of many of the Swiss cantons. The male peasant dons a simple goat-skin, very wide knickerbockers, linen leggings, sandals, and red cap or hat with a broad brim.

Near to Palma is a fine old stone pile of Moorish fashion, built by Don Jayme I. (El Conquistador), to commemorate the conquest of Majorca; and, further on, occupying a fine position amongst orange-groves, and upon a gentle slope overlooking the Mediterranean, is Bendinat, the handsome palace of the Marqués de Romano; so called in Catalan, or old Provençal, from the fact of the Conquistador having *dined well* on that spot after he gained his victory.

The language of the island is Mallorquin, which is simply a slight corruption of Catalan. The Catalan language and the old Provençal were, at the period of the conquest of Barcelona from the Moors, nearly identical. It was introduced into the Baleares by the King of Aragon, Don Jayme, at the period of his conquest of Majorca. As, however, education has of late made great progress in these islands, no less than on the mainland, and is conducted upon excellent principles, the classical language of Spain, the pure Castilian, is now everywhere taught, and the teaching of provincial patois is prohibited. The connection of the crown of Aragon with that of Castile having formed the basis of the Spanish monarchy, it will be easily understood how the two languages, the Castilian and the Catalan, are, in a great measure, blended together. The Castilian, however, while still preserving its high finish, purity, and elegance, owes much of its force to the bold, nervous tongue of the old warlike race of Aragon.

As one wanders through the narrow streets of Palma, he remarks frequent vestiges of the Saracenic period, besides many sombre mediæval palaces of Gothic architecture grafted on the Moorish style, in perfect preservation, forming of themselves cool, well-shaded streets. Their *façades* are fretted with arabesque devices borrowed from the East, while the armorial bearings of their once knightly or merchant possessors still indicate by whom they were occupied. Their tall, arched windows are all supported by twisted pillarets, while the ornate sky-lines are generally battlemented. We peered beneath many low, broad archways in these narrow, silent streets, as we passed along, and discovered several elegant square *patios* and marble courts, with carved fountains in the midst, the spray from which diffused a delightful coolness. Around the four walls of these courts are arcaded terraces, canopied with arches crossing and recrossing each other, and rising from light spiral columns of the most elegant appearance; while the whole is supported beneath by greater and nobler arches of rare device, resting on massive columns, with shaft and capital chased with rich and elaborate carving. The evidence of great former opulence is found throughout the city in the splendid relics of Saracenic architecture, or in those numerous palaces of vast size, with their marble staircases and traceried balustrades. The magnificent relics of the past tell plainly of the once flourishing condition of Majorca and its capital, whether as the home of the Moor, as the abode and settlement of the numerous knightly followers of the royal conqueror, Don Jayme, or as the residence of luxurious merchant princes who made this fair isle their home and the dépôt of their argosies, at the period when the Baleares were in the full highway to the gorgeous East, before Vasco da Gama had discovered the route to the Indies by the Cape of Good Hope. [27] Buildings of surpassing beauty—especially the Lonja, overlooking the harbour, once the exchange, or *bourse*, and place of public meeting of these busy communities, and the style of which is the most exquisite Gothic—attest the former combination of taste and opulence existing amongst them.

Amidst the habitations of the lower classes we always found the modern buildings raised upon the broken ruins of Moorish structures; and the substrata of Moorish masonry never having been reduced to any general level, there is an aspect of inequality, a rise and fall in all the lines of the town, from whatever point it be observed, which is most picturesque. Valetta, perhaps, is the only other city whose general appearance is similar in this respect. Decay, however, is speeding on with rapid though stealthy pace, and these remnants of the past must soon disappear.

The city is surrounded by fortifications; but the most modern in use—those of Philip II.—though still massive, would be, notwithstanding the show of garrison within, as effete against an enemy as the Saracenic works, now crumbling away, upon which they are built.

Although visited by occasional tempests, which gather amongst the highlands and sweep over the island, Majorca enjoys a most luxuriant climate. The sun looks down throughout the year from a heaven of serenest blue. The great heat of the southern summer is tempered by the fresh sea breeze, and the verdant mountain slopes and valleys offer a cool and shady protection from the rays of a powerful sun. The soil of the plains is rich, and, cultivated by the industry of the hardy island race, yields most luxuriant crops of corn and flax, while the orange, olive, and the carob grow in the wildest luxuriance.

During the summer there is a great scarcity of water; but the rains of autumn and winter are collected for the irrigation of the land in enormous reservoirs, which contain sufficient water to last throughout the dry season. Each landholder has his fields then flooded in turn, at certain intervals, upon payment of a water-rate. The fertility of the island, coupled with the honesty and industry of the inhabitants, renders living cheap; and beyond the walls of the semi-Spanish capital, extortion, even in the faintest form, is unknown throughout the length and breadth of Majorca.

The peasantry and the owners of the soil live on terms of the greatest amity and contentment. The distinction of class is recognised in no way that produces the slightest bitterness or heartburnings. For long years the happy islanders, separated from the rest of the world, have regarded each other as one family. They seem to care little, and even to know little, of other nations, or even of the country of which their island is one of the provinces. Absorbed in their patriarchal mode of existence, estranged in their habits and mode of life from their fellow-subjects of the peninsula, the simple islanders know nothing of the want, the sufferings, and the crimes which have too frequently thrown a gloom over the history of larger, more enlightened, and more civilised communities.

In this small and peaceful island each one regards his neighbour with a trust that is rarely betrayed. There is a constant state of contentment, disturbed by no unreasonable desires. Humble competence, won by honest labour, well and persistently done, is all that is necessary to satisfy these simple people.

FOOTNOTES:

[25] Mallorca, in Spanish.

[26] Ancient King of Majorca. Son of Jayme I., King of Aragon, called *El Conquistador*, from having conquered Majorca from the Moors, A.D. 1229.

[27] A.D. 1498.

CHAPTER XII.

THE VALE OF SOLLER.—CHARACTER OF THE PEOPLE.—INTRODUCTION OF THE TELEGRAPH.—SUPERSTITION OF THE PEASANTRY.—PRODUCTIONS OF THE ISLAND.—THE ROAD.—GUARDIA CIVIL.—OBLIGING LANDLADY.—BRIDGE OF LA MÀ.—BATTLE WITH THE TURKS.

THE Vale of Soller, some thirty miles across the island, is the most delightful excursion the tourist can make. As, of course, we had resolved to visit it, behold us twisting round the sharp corners of the narrow streets of Palma in an open carriage, drawn by a team of four splendid mules at full gallop, with the driver's whip keeping up a running fire, and the driver himself uttering volleys of yells, while the people in the street flew right and left like parting waters, and a crowd of yelping dogs pursued us. After rattling through an old Moorish arch, and over a drawbridge, we dashed into the open country. In a short time we came upon a region of gigantic olive-trees. Many centuries must have fallen upon them, for they were grey and hoar. Some of the great gnarled trunks, fifteen feet in circumference, were twisted and tortured by wayward nature into a thousand weird and uncouth shapes. These wonderful trees, old when the Moor ruled the island, have outlived many a change in its history. Since their birth, whole peoples have become dust, and dynasties have passed away. They are relics of a younger world; and as twilight falls around them, they loom with their long, lean arms and distorted trunks, gaunt and ghastly, against the dull grey air, like an assembly of ancient ghosts.

From this scene we emerged into wide plains, green with sprouting corn, and bordered by gigantic aloes. These plains yield three crops a year. On jog the jingling mules, while the clouds of yellow dust whirl away in the morning breeze. We pass pretty flat-roofed, Oriental-looking houses, with coloured blinds and balconies, buried in groves of acacia and prickly pear. We were saluted on our way by many a dark-eyed maid, hooded in her gauzy capote, and with the one long plait of hair, or by stalwart labourers as they walked briskly to their day's work.

There were other peasants working in the fields, dressed in long, loose Turkish trousers and bright sash, their heads bound in gaudy kerchiefs, who all paused from their labour to wave a greeting as we passed, and to cry, "Tenga, Señores, tenga." [28] In character, these good people are the reverse of their neighbours of Valencia or Catalonia. They are so simple and honest, that crime in Majorca is a great exception; while in Valencia it is dangerous to walk abroad after dark without some weapon of defence, and that, of course, is useless against the assassin who approaches from behind. In this homely isle one may wander about as much as he pleases, in the alleys of the city or amidst the mountain passes, secure and unmolested. There are few or no means of escape for the criminal, and, therefore, his detection is certain, for the people refuse him all shelter. Majorcans eagerly desire to maintain peace and order in their island, and crime is, therefore, rendered a losing game.

The Majorcan peasants, however, are superstitious to a degree, and densely ignorant. This may be accounted for by the fact that the mass of the population consists of the labouring classes, and that they are so completely isolated from the rest of mankind. To attempt, therefore, to engraft upon their primitive minds any scientific or artistic improvement is an unfruitful task. A few years ago a line of telegraphic communication was attempted between Soller and Palma; but as soon as the poles and wires were erected, they were in many places destroyed, not from wilful malice, but from a fixed notion that the telegraph was some diabolical invention of the Evil One, destined to bring them to any amount of grief. It was in vain to expostulate or explain. The wires were cut and cut again. However, upon the magnetic principle being made known to the peasantry of the district, some more enlightened than the rest wished to test its efficacy by positive proof; and when they heard that messages might be sent along the wires, they concluded that goods and chattels might be transported in the same manner from place to place. Consequently, during the first week after the telegraph had commenced operations, all sorts of things were found hanging on the wires for a distance of nearly five miles—bundles of clothes, pairs of knickerbockers, petticoats, baskets of edibles, and even wigs. In fact, an *olla podrida* of domestic articles, all neatly ticketed and addressed, was found waving in the breeze. The good peasantry, however, finding that the telegraph was longer in its transmission of these articles to their destination than they had anticipated, naturally concluded that the whole thing was a hoax and a swindle on the part of the Government and Satan, and wreaked their vengeance upon the unfortunate poles and wires by knocking them down.

We had approached to the foot of the mountain range we had hitherto seen from afar, to which the road ascended by gradual inclines. The higher we wound from the heat below, the sharper became the breeze. On all sides Alpine vegetation spread around, perfuming the air with a hundred odours. We pursued the zig-zags until we were enclosed by a semicircle of enormous precipices and stupendous rocks, on whose beetling brows the toppling fir-trees clung. We felt overwhelmed by the sight of these stupendous masses, for it seemed as if a breath would dislodge them, and hurl them down upon us. The road, escaping for a time from the deep recesses of these adamantine walls, skirted the level edge of a lofty precipice; and, on one occasion, we splashed through a torrent which, a few feet on our left, fell in a wide arch over the rocky margin, and rushed, silvering in the sunny air, far down into the dark gulf beneath, while the roar of its waters echoed like distant thunder amongst the hollows of the desolate mountains. Again we ascended, and in proportion as we rose, the peaks seemed to rear themselves above us. Then we dived into a vast enclosure of vertical walls, in which we felt as if in a prison, deep and gloomy itself, but from which we could see the bright vault of heaven above.

After an hour's climb in this sombre valley, we sat down for rest and a *cigarillo* on a way-side stone to await the coming of the mules and carriage. As we looked back through the rocky pass by which we had entered the gorge, we had a pleasant, though far distant, view of light green slopes and wide spreading plains, shining brightly in the yellow glow of day, and occasionally tinted with the grey hues of the olive. Bounding these plains, in a long narrow line of dazzling light, were the white walls of Palma; while beyond, its hue contrasting with the transparent blue of the spotless sky, and flecked here and there by the white sail of the feluccas, quivered the long high line of the purple sea. Higher yet we ascend, over roads paved by the Moors six hundred years ago. Leaving the carriage on the path below, we scramble up through tangled shrubberies, through cactus, aloes, carob, evergreen oak, and ancient olive. All around and over us are piled the wild mountains, with forests of pine scaling to their very peaks, and standing out like funeral plumes in dark, black fringes against the radiant sky. We pass groups of strong sunburnt peasants, with a simple goat-skin tied upon their backs for a garment. We perceive among them timid girls, large-eyed and hooded, with streaming plaits of blue-black or golden auburn hair, and old women, squatting on mules, with their heads covered by the hat, or masculine head-gear, like that worn by the women of Wales. Wider and wider, as we rise above the lower landscape, spreads the glorious prospect behind us—wild rock, verdant slope, sunny plains, streaked with the dusky olive, the long, white line of the distant city, and the dark blue breast of the dreaming sea; until, of a sudden, we pass over a dark rocky plateau, and the scene drops quickly from view, like the dreams of boyhood, the bright yearnings of youth, and all things of beauty which are born to fade,—

"Youth's fond dreams, like evening skies,

Are tinged with colours bright;

Their cloud-built walls and turrets rise

In lines of dazzling light.

"But Time wears on with stealthy pace,

And robes of solemn grey,

And in the shadow of its face,

The glories fade away."

But a truce to moralising, or we shall never get on with the journey.

We pass over the rocky plateau, and everything behind us, as we begin our descent, is totally eclipsed. In advance, deep and far below, resting in the very lap of one vast chaos of wild and lofty mountains, lies the white little town of Soller. Its scattered groups of toy-like houses are gleaming from out the dark-green of orange groves and bowers of citron. The long declines of the yellow road appear, from our elevated position, to wind away into the distant foliage like golden serpents. All around rise giant rocks, and enormous blocks, reft by the lightning from their parent walls, hang threatening on the very verge of lofty cliffs high above us; while the great azure circle cut out of heaven by the vast coronet of peaks which, at a great altitude aloft, sweeps round the scene, is clear and spotless, save where an eagle poised on level wing is bathing in the balmy air. Down rattles the calèche, and the four black mules jingle merrily on. Turn after turn is made in the road, and rock and gorge assume wilder proportions, until on a sudden the enormous peak of the Puig Mayor, the loftiest mountain in Majorca, is seen towering upwards in gloomy majesty over the fair scene below.

As we descended we breathed a warmer atmosphere, and at last found ourselves in the fragrant valley of Soller, in the very heart of its green and fruitful bosom, where the air was heavy with the odour of the orange-flower, and the fig in profusion purpled on the tree. We threaded lane after lane, shaded over with the deep green branches which met overhead, the golden fruit hanging from them in festoons, and temptingly inviting us to pluck them. The whole country around seemed like a wide garden, in the midst of which waved palms and pampas-grass. There was everywhere a richness of verdure, a profusion of life, which showed the fecundity of nature in these Southern climes. The charm of the scenery was much increased by the contrast between the savage mountains, so bare and rocky, and the perfect paradise which nature in her benigner moments had created in every valley. [29]

The village of Soller is a credit to the Spanish nation and to itself. Spain and its towns are dirty and malodorous, sanitary laws being generally neglected; but here, in this remote corner of her dominions, lying unknown and buried in a deep mountain basin, and secluded from the rest of the world, she possesses a beautiful little village, remarkable for the cleanliness of its houses and people. At Soller, as everywhere throughout the island, there is a decency of deportment, a respect for law, a modesty and urbanity of demeanor which it is really delightful to witness.

The interior of the little inn, or *posada*—which means literally a place of repose—is washed and whitewashed, scrubbed and polished, until it is as free from speck or stain as the far-famed Dutch villages which are held up to the Great Unwashed at large as sanitary and salutary examples. The little trestle bedsteads of white wood, with their snowy sheets, in the little whitewashed bedrooms, seem in their happy ignorance of the flea to put completely to the blush those foul and noisome beds in Spanish inns in which the wearied traveller lies down, not to find repose, but to offer himself a helpless victim to myriads of enemies, who from every nook and cranny come forth, thirsting for his blood.

The valley of Soller, only six miles in circumference, realizes £25,000 per annum by the sale of its oranges and lemons, and £30,000 by its oil. The olive trees grow luxuriantly everywhere, and on terraces cut out of the slopes of the mountains are nursed into the highest perfection. The roads are in excellent condition, and so much engineering skill has been displayed in their construction that the transit of fruit over the mountains to the port of embarkation is a comparatively easy matter. All the roads, the mountain passes, and the island generally, are protected, although from the character of the Majorcans the precaution is scarcely necessary, by a fine body of police, called the *Guardia Civil*. They are a manly, robust body of men, numbering eleven thousand, including those who are employed on the entire eastern coast of the mainland, a comparatively small number being required in the islands. In many parts of Spain proper, brigandage exists to a considerable extent, and the whole force is therefore ordered to parade their allotted districts with loaded carbines. In Majorca their offices, as we have said, are little needed, but on the mainland their interference is often requisite, and they perform their arduous duties with all the rigour necessary for the maintenance of law amongst the daring races who inhabit the mountains and sea-coasts of Spain. If anyone who is discovered in the act of setting the law at defiance refuses to surrender, he is shot down without mercy. These intrepid men have often to maintain most unequal struggles, and are, of course, held in great detestation amongst the criminal classes, by whom they are frequently made victims to their thirst for vengeance. Their uniform is picturesque, yet workmanlike, consisting precisely of the costume of the popular Italian brigand without his tawdry finery.

The great charm of the Majorcan population is that they are a distinct island race, with a language almost of their own; and having lived for centuries happily and contentedly as one family, they are docile and orderly, and courteous to a degree to strangers. Steam has only been introduced of late years, and up to the first arrival of *El Vapor* they were comparatively cut off from all the world, its plots and passions, and engrossed in their own quiet industrious pursuits.

Majorca is at present free from the plague of tourists. Scarcely a stranger intrudes, beyond the city of Palma, into the recesses of its woods, mountains, and villages. Consequently the charge for everything is remarkably moderate, and on the occasion of our excursion to Soller we had a capital dinner for five people, [30] including a sack of four hundred oranges fresh from the boughs, for ten shillings, besides a deal of stroking, and patting, and shaking of hands on the part of the "fair, fat, and forty" landlady, her daughter, and mine host of the Fonda de la Paz, upon our departure for the mountain pass of El Barranco. The good landlady, who is also cook, we understood danced a characteristic dance some twelve years ago before Lord L——e, on his visit to Soller, like the daughter of Herodias before Herod. Being at the time of our visit of sufficient dimensions to put up in the middle of a room for an invalid to walk ten times round in the course of a day, as a measurement for a term of gentle exercise, that lady very properly abstained from repeating her Terpsichorean experiments upon this occasion. Had she given way to her love of the graceful exercise, she would have borne no very distant resemblance to a frisky elephant, and might probably have broken through the floor of the apartment.

From the *mirador*, or pretty terrace on the top of the house, entwined with vine-leaves and jasmine, and partly shaded with the fig and various sweet-scented plants, a lovely view of well-nigh the entire valley, with its mass of vegetable life, its wide orange groves, and its waving palms, is obtained, while the fragrance of the orange flower is wafted through every casement. The winter climate of the valley is mild and delicious, as its tropical vegetation amply testifies; while the heat in summer is never too intense, for an opening through the heart of the mountains towards the north-west, through which a small silver river flows to the sea, admits the freshening breeze.

From Soller we started on a beautiful walk to the port (El Puerto de Soller), situated on the north-west coast. The road lay through orange groves, and avenues of gigantic bamboos and enormous aloes, the little river flowing swiftly on by our side. When we had advanced some distance an old battered bridge appeared before us. This was the bridge of La Má, where in the middle of the sixteenth century a fearful struggle, accompanied with great slaughter, occurred between a host of invading Turks and the gallant men of Soller. The inhabitants of the little town, although greatly outnumbered, were nerved by the energy of despair, and it was a question of "to do or die." They must either conquer or leave their old men, their wives, their kindred, and little ones to enemies who knew no mercy, but would certainly doom them to dishonour, death, or slavery. Arming themselves, therefore, hastily with whatever weapons they could collect, the little band of six hundred [31] knelt down in the market-place and prayed fervently to the God of the Christians to bless their arms. Then, committing their families to the care of heaven, they marched to the attack. The Turkish army, having landed at three o'clock in the morning, had imagined they could take the town by surprise, while its inhabitants were sunk in slumber; but their fleet had been previously seen in the offing by the Majorcans from their watch-tower at the port, and signalled to the Soller garrison. At the bridge of La Má the opposing forces met, and the battle raged with equal ardour on both sides. In the midst of the struggle a rumour reached the Christian troops that another band of Turks had appeared near their town by a circuitous route, and were slaughtering their families and firing their homes. This sad message for a moment fell upon their hearts like a knell of despair, and for a short time they were so dispirited that the Turks gained some temporary advantage. At this critical moment the calm, quick wisdom of Juan Angelats, the patriot leader, saw that upon one supreme effort depended the issue of the day. Leaping upon a mound, with the banner of the Red Cross of St. George waving in his hand, and in full sight of both armies, with bare head and flaming eyes, he shouted, "Sons of Soller! if we retire we are scattered and lost. Rally, rally! Our families are in the hands of God. Charge for vengeance and Saint George, and let not an infidel escape. Forward, in the name of the Holy Virgin!" With one loud shout the gallant band rushed on with the impetuous speed of a vast bolt discharged upon the foe. Nothing could withstand the violence of their assault, and crossing the river over the heap of Turkish dead, they spread death and destruction among the Mohammedan troops, being resolved neither to ask nor to give quarter. Ysuf, the enemy's leader, fell pierced through and through, and the falling ranks of the infidels, dropping victims at every step in their retreat, fled in wild disorder to their galleys; only one-fourth of the invaders eventually landing at Algiers to attest the prowess of the Christian patriot.

Shortly after passing the bridge of La Má we arrived at the port of Soller, formed by a little bay, at the entrance of which, on either side, rise lofty rocks, covered with olive, and with patches of dwarf oak, while occasional pines wave their sombre heads gloomily in the breeze. It is a wild and desolate place, the only sound which is heard being that of the blue waves as they dash ceaselessly on the silent shore. A ruined Moorish tower rises up, stark and grey, on the storm-battered rocks, like some melancholy spirit brooding over recollections of the past. A few small fishing craft, which are all that seek refuge here, sway to-and-fro, moored to the shore, beneath some humble cottages overlooking the low wall of the little harbour. The bay itself is to all intents fathomless, being the basin of an extinct volcano, and there is consequently no anchorage for ships.

FOOTNOTES:

[28] The usual passing form of salutation in Majorca. It means "good day," or "good night," or anything civil in fact.

[29] There may be some who will suspect this account of an almost unknown but comparatively near island to be exaggerated. To such we say, some day, instead of going to Geneva, go to Majorca.

[30] We were accompanied by Captain Graham, Her Majesty's Consul at Palma; Captain Wood, R.N., and Mrs. Wood. To all of them we are indebted for the greatest kindness and courtesy shown to us during our stay in Majorca.

[31] Strange to say—the number of the gallant few who rode at Balaclava.

CHAPTER XIII.

THE PORT OF SOLLER.—CONVENT OF LLUCH.—A LEGEND OF THE MONASTERY.—CATHEDRAL OF PALMA.—REMAINS OF KING JAYME II.—ATTRACTIONS OF THE BALEARIC ISLES.—MINORCA.—ITS CONNECTION WITH ENGLISH HISTORY.

THE walks around Soller are varied and beautiful, presenting to the delighted eye a charming blending of savage wildness and fertile cultivation. In no part of the world can one behold a more complete picture-gallery of all the varieties of natural scenery than in the Isle of Majorca. The day following our arrival at Soller was warm and radiant, as, indeed, every day appears to be in this favoured spot. After a breakfast of fresh figs, new milk, and a stew of pigeons and rice, we started through the orange-gardens to the mountains. The morning air was so warm and fragrant that, as it gently fanned us, we felt as if we were in a perfumed bath, until we stepped upon the first incline of the rocky slopes, where, as we were under the shade of immense rocks, the atmosphere was colder. Sometimes we found ourselves in great chasms where the mountain appeared to have been rent asunder by some violent explosion of the forces of nature; and when, occasionally alarmed by a sharp and piercing cry, we looked upwards, we saw the lordly eagle with outstretched wings hovering over the abyss.

After ascending a steep path winding between perpendicular walls of rock, we came suddenly upon a scene of great grandeur, lonely, dark, and gloomy. Away in our front a mighty ravine, cleft by some great throe of nature, yawned to such an enormous depth that it seemed to disclose the very core of the mountain. While standing on the verge of a narrow pathway, the eye, as it looked over it, plunged down into a great abyss of darkness, from which, far below, arose black towers of rock and broken pinnacles looming in the rising mists. It made the senses reel to fancy, if the foot slipped, or the edge of the pathway gave way, to what unknown recesses of the earth we should descend! High above were tossed, like the giant waves of a granite sea, a wild chaos of dark and lofty peaks, while, over all, stern in its grand and gloomy majesty, frowned against the bright blue sky the vast black head of the Puig Mayor. [32]

This splendid gorge, which, as a specimen of the grandeur of mountain solitudes must be one of the most characteristic in Europe, is called El Barranco. [33] When one stands alone in such a scene—far removed from all familiar associations—it is almost impossible to describe in any language that would not be deemed extravagant, the sensation by which he is overpowered. From the summit of the Puig, the magnificence of the prospect will repay a good walker for the trouble of the ascent. Raised high above a region of mountain peaks, black stupendous gorges, and a wild chaos of riven rocks, shot up from the bowels of the globe in some primeval convulsion, soars the massive summit. While we were standing on it we watched the afternoon sun slow wheeling down to the westward seas. Immediately beneath, fantastic clouds and long weird streaks of vapour curled and eddied like strange aërial phantoms amongst the solemn recesses of the lonely mountains, sinking into the darkness of the vast depths below.

Over the wide plains of the island stretched like a giant's chart at our feet, green savannahs, broad dusky tracts of olive, and expanses of yellow sand, sparkling here and there in all directions, were exhibited to our delighted gaze. Towns surrounded by glittering white walls, and scattered hamlets peeping from out the deep recesses of spreading woods and groves of orange, greeted the wondering eye; while away towards the horizon, encircling the magnificent prospect, was the sea, flecked in all directions with tiny sunlit sails.

After scrambling down the great mountain walls, when the shades of night began to gather around us, we descended to the Convent of Lluch, which we reached, thanks to our wary guide, in safety. The wild tracks and narrow paths, sometimes skirting precipices of enormous depth, naturally suggested thoughts of danger. In some formidable gaps of the mountain there was nothing but the dull twilight and the deep sapphire of the skies to light us on our narrow way; and, had it not been for the implicit reliance we placed in our practised guide, the heart of the bravest might well have quailed. We two Englishmen, plodding on at night in the steps of a wild mountaineer, guided only by the occasional gleam of his cigarette, among the lonely crags of the Majorcan hills, were conscious of a certain romantic pleasure which we experienced in contemplating the novelty and danger of our position.

We slept that night at the Convent of Lluch, a lonely place in a hollow of the mountain. A forlorn-looking and cadaverous young man, in a long garment of neutral tint, and with a greasy black angular cap on his head, opened the door when we rang for admittance. His reception of us was rather peculiar. After yawning and scratching himself, he turned his back and went into the building, looking very like Noah going into the ark, as popularly delineated in the familiar toy in vogue amongst British infants. He, however, returned in a moment, with a candle which shed a watery gleam on the bare walls, and ushered us into the convent, where we were entertained in a rather frugal manner.

After discussing, at the extreme end of a very long table, in a very long room, and in a very short time, a repast of sour wine, like very inferior African port, with black bread and hard eggs, tasting as if they had been boiled in lamp-oil, we retired to rest in a bare, whitewashed cell, where we slept upon a couple of mattresses, covered over with striped woollen mule rugs. We observed in our chamber, hanging on a nail, a very depressing picture of some saint or other with a catherine-wheel apparently exploding from the back of a very bald head. The Convent of Lluch, or Luke, is celebrated as a place where the Virgin, at some former period, descended from Heaven. She came only once, we were told, and considering all things, we really cannot wonder at her having found one visit quite sufficient.

After our fatiguing climb amongst the mountains, we were glad to find ourselves again in the sunny city of Palma, with its old carved gateways, its yellow, flat-roofed houses, dusty roads, acacia avenues, picturesque population, and Damascus-like scenes. It was pleasant to retire from the blaze of the midday sun into the cool shade of old Gothic cloisters, with their beautiful pillars and arches. We wandered with delight in the bright green garden in the midst, or strayed at will into half-ruined courtyards, with grand old Moorish arches, offering a dim and silent retreat. Everything in the city has an Oriental character. The numerous actual remains of Saracenic architecture, the splendid mansions built by mediæval knights or merchants, the yellow walls on which the aloe grows, and the arched windows here and there perched in picturesque irregularity, or looking down into gardens filled with palms, cacti, and feathery shrubs, all remind one of the East.

The cathedral, a noble pile, was commenced in 1230, by Don Jayme, and finished in 1346. Standing on an elevated position overlooking the sea, its heavy mass, with all its great buttresses and flying arches, is seen from some distance. Below are the broad stone ramparts, and on either side the beautiful Bay of Palma stretches towards it its long azure arms. At the present moment, extensive repairs and additions are being made, and a magnificent *façade* is to be erected at its western extremity; but, to our eyes, the garish brightness of the new stone contrasts unpleasantly with the time-honoured grey of its grand old walls, which have stood in all their majesty through so many centuries.

The interior, as we enter, makes a great and solemn impression upon the mind. The light of day reaches the holy space tempered and subdued by windows of stained glass; and the noble height of the nave seems doubly lofty from being supported by pillars not of heavy and clumsy breadth, but of graceful and delicate proportions.

The choir, as usual in Spanish cathedrals, is situated in the very centre of the building. Although magnificent in itself, it interferes with the otherwise imposing length of the whole interior, and seems like a great mass of lumber, carelessly left on the pavement, which one would have gladly swept away, in order that the beautiful perspective and the architectural proportions might be rendered distinctly visible. With its lofty aisles, its slender columns, and coloured windows, it has some resemblance to Westminster Abbey, without the ugly statues.

Within a marble sarcophagus near the choir is the body of Don Jayme II., King of Majorca, and son of the Conquistador, Don Jayme I.; and anyone, upon the payment of a few reals, may minutely inspect all that remains of that ancient personage. A spring is touched, a panel of the tomb opens, and a long glass case or coffin is pulled out, and rested on a trestle. Dressed in royal robes of scarlet, gold, and ermine, the wrinkled, grinning corpse of the King of Majorca is exhibited as a spectacle. The bones are protruding through the brown leather-like hide, and piercing the embroidered gloves. The mouth is stretched widely open, showing a dark chasm within, guarded by three long teeth, shaking in the jaw as the glass coffin is moved. The round sockets, where once sparkled the proud and kingly eyes, are now receptacles for dust and a dead fly or two; while a few grisly hairs escape from under the velvet cap which covers the skull. The ears, shrivelled into bits of dried parchment, stick out on either side of the head like those of a monkey. Pieces of tanned flesh hang here and there by slender fibres, in some places peeling off the throat and face, and leaving dark little pits beneath. This is all that remains of a once noble king; and to the complexion of being made a shocking peep-show for the morbid herd of modern gapers, has Don Jayme Segundo come at last. We join in the prayer, *Requiescat in pace*, inscribed on his tomb; but whether in such circumstances he can be said to do so is more than doubtful.

It has often struck me as very surprising that, seeing there is so much throughout this lovely Mediterranean isle to interest the mind in a hundred various ways, so much to ravish the eye, and such a climate for the ailing and the sick, not to speak of the attractions of its chief city, no mention has hitherto been made of Majorca in the guide-books of the day. In fact, Messrs. Bradshaw and Murray ought, without delay, to make reparations for their past neglect; for truly there are no parts of the coast of the Mediterranean Sea—no isles on its bosom—more attractive to the tourist than these Spanish dependencies. Irrespective of the beauties and interest of Majorca, one would think the fact that the island of Minorca had for a certain period been connected with the history of England would be sufficient to warrant the bestowal of more attention on the Balearic Isles.

Port Mahon, too, one of the finest harbours in the world, is situated in Minorca.

The name of this island, as all know, is also sadly associated with that of one of our naval heroes, Admiral John Byng. It was to the relief of Minorca from the French that Byng was dispatched on that expedition which ended in results so unfortunate for himself. Although a brave, gallant seaman, highly distinguished for his knowledge of naval matters, the tactics of this commander were ever those of caution, and his hesitation to attack a fleet of far superior force, and risk the reputation of his country by possible, if not probable, defeat, excited great odium against him. Upon the intelligence of the cautious manner in which he had conducted his operations becoming known in England, the Ministry, too feeble and cowardly to bear honestly the consequences of their own mistaken measures, threw the entire blame upon the Admiral, and roused afresh the anger of the nation against him by accusing him of cowardice. He was tried by court-martial, and, although recommended to mercy, was condemned to be shot. He met his fate with calm heroism at Portsmouth, March 14th, 1757, and, by his demeanour in his last moments, put to shame the miserable calumnies of his accusers.

"How many traitors to their God and King

Escape the death which was reserved for Byng."

FOOTNOTES:

[32] The loftiest mountain in the island—4850 feet above the sea.

[33] The Ravine.

CHAPTER XIV.

HOW TO STUDY SPANISH CHARACTER.—BULL-FIGHTS.—PROVISION FOR THE SPIRITUAL WELFARE OF BULL-FIGHTERS.—FIGHT BETWEEN AN ELEPHANT AND A BULL.—EXPEDITION TO THE CAVES OF ARTÀ.

BULL-FIGHTS, although we are told they are condemned by the priests, are still the fashion in Spain. They are the national *fiesta*, and to see the Spanish public in their natural characteristics one must go to these tumultuous scenes, as the "intelligent foreigner" is supposed to go to the Derby to comprehend the nature of the free-born Briton. The best bull-fights [34] are to be seen at Seville, that favoured city having the first pick of the noble bulls which are bred only in Andaluçia.

The season commences on the first Sunday after Lent, and, weather permitting, a *funcion* comes off each succeeding Sunday. During the intense heat of Midsummer there is an interval, but the sports are resumed at the end of August, continuing to the latter part of October, after which period the cold weather seems to exercise a depressing influence on the energy of the animal, preventing the full fury of the bullish nature from being aroused, and so renders this hero of the Spanish arena incapable of showing fight. The expense of each *corrida* is about £400 in the larger cities.

The spiritual welfare of the bull-fighters is always provided for at each *funcion*. Behind the scenes an altar is erected with burning candles, and a priest is ever in waiting to shrive any wounded man who may be carried dying out of the ring.

Common as may be descriptions of bull-fights to the world at large, we believe a *corrida*, which we had an opportunity of witnessing, has never been described before. It was a fight between an elephant and four bulls. The proprietor of the former animal was a Frenchman, who, inspired with the idea that such a novel combat would reinvigorate the palling taste of the public for scenes of slaughter, had bought an elephant, and, at an enormous outlay in loaves of bread and hay, not to speak of fresh water, was conducting him through the Spanish dominions with a challenge to all comers, in the way of bulls, to mortal combat—just as gentlemen of sporting tastes, with tight trousers, fur caps, and mufflers, go from place to place in England with a bull-terrier, backing him to kill so many rats a day.

We soon found our way, along with a babbling crowd, to the great white amphitheatre without the city, and seated ourselves on one of the benches which sloped up from the arena. The spectators consisted of the usual motley garlic-smelling multitude. All were smoking cigarillos, and, with flashing eyes awaited the commencement of the exciting spectacle. Within the circle below, and opposite to the doors which admit the bull, stood a noble elephant with long white tusks. A bright red cloth was thrown across his back, and while his small eyes seemed to survey, with a mild expression, the scene before him, he employed his time in breaking up loaves of bread, which, with the aid of his trunk, he deposited safely in his huge body—an operation which he performed apparently with much calm enjoyment.

The people of Majorca had evidently never seen an elephant before, and many were their speculations as to the nature and characteristics of the animal. One pretty young woman, with a *rebosiño*, lace mittens, and night-black tresses, who was sitting next to us, had but very confused notions as to which was the trunk and which the tail of the strange creature at which she looked with eyes flashing with wonder and curiosity. An excited youth cried out directly he saw it, "Caramba! why, the beast has got two tails!"

When the large circle within the walls was filled with the swaying crowd, and while the buzz of expectation hummed around, the blast of a trumpet was suddenly heard, and, with a loud bang, the wooden gates flew open, and in cantered, with lashing tail and glowing eye, the heavy form of the bull. For a moment he arrested his course, and looked round as if for an enemy, at the same time pawing the ground impatiently. Almost immediately he caught sight of the strange beast on the opposite side of the ring, dressed in the hated red cloth, quietly munching his loaves of bread. Greek had now met Greek, and fierce was expected to be the tug of war. As quick as lightning the levelled horns went down, and the bull rushed in full career upon the elephant. The struggle was short, for in three seconds the bull fell dead upon the sand, pierced completely through the chest to his heart, having, in the fury of his onset, impaled himself upon the long sharp tusks of his mighty foe.

The elephant, upon seeing the bull enter, simply kept his small eyes fixed upon him, and stood firm and fast on his four great pillars of legs, like some strong castle from which his tusks protruded like spears. The shock of his meeting with the bull came with a crash that made the very walls vibrate sensibly; and after the short but fearful efforts of the latter, which had no more effect upon his opponent than a wave upon a rock, the body of the assailant was hurled back, pierced by those formidable weapons of offence with which nature has endowed the elephant. After rebounding from the force with which he was hurled back, the bull rolled over and settled in a broad lake of blood.

Bravo, elefante! was the shout which rose enthusiastically from a thousand throats to congratulate the elephant on the victory which he had obtained.

That peaceful but formidable animal, unmindful of their applause, resumed the operation in which he had been interrupted, applying himself again to the consumption of his loaves as unconcernedly as if he had merely knocked off some troublesome fly.

From this passage of arms the enormous strength and weight of the greatest beast of creation could in a moment be discerned. So firmly, so steadily did he maintain his position that he scarcely moved as the bull, vast in his own proportions, threw himself upon his opponent with all the impetus with which rage and fury could inspire him. The amount of exertion which the elephant expended in the affair appeared to the onlookers to be wonderfully small. In galloped the gaudy mules, and, as they wheeled gaily round, the iron hook at their heels was adjusted, and the gory carcase was in an instant swept away from the arena.

Another bull was then admitted. After a pause he perceived his opponent, and, with the blind rage of his nature, rushed furiously at him. A cloud of dust rose in the air at the place where the two beasts met, and a loud bellowing was heard to issue from it. A struggle, as of giants, continued for a few seconds. When, at last, the spectators succeeded in perceiving what had taken place, it was seen that the tusk of the elephant had entered into the eye of the bull, and had become fixed for a moment in the skull. The rage of the maddened beast was fearful to behold as he rolled and fell. Leaping from the ground he dashed his two fore-feet violently against the elephant's forehead, but the hard substance of his skull remained uninjured. The scene was, in fact, so horrid—though one's gaze was kept fixed upon it as by a spell—that it will not admit of minute description.

It was a relief when the fearful contest was brought to an end. One blow of the elephant's foot, which descended with a loud thud, beat in the chest of the martyred bull; and, as the agonised brute reeled sobbing to earth, his enormous enemy dropped upon him in a kneeling posture and simply crushed him to death. Another victory! *Bravo, elefante!* was again shouted with more enthusiasm than before. Fresh sand was thrown upon the bloody arena, and the surviving monster, unhurt save by a few light flesh wounds here and there, stood once again gloomily aside, swinging his proboscis slowly to and fro, or blowing up the sand into little eddies as he quietly smelt with it along the ground. Notwithstanding the horrors of the spectacle we have, as yet, only partially described, the accessories were really brilliant. Crowds of beautiful ladies applauded the successful combatant. Fans were waving in all directions, and the dazzling rays of the sun were reflected by flashing jewels and laughing eyes.

While the hubbub of excited voices mingled with the cries of water-sellers, another blast of the trumpet pealed out, and, in a moment, a gigantic bull rushed across the ring. As if descrying by instinct the destroyer of his companions, he dashed impetuously upon the elephant, with such blind ferocity that horns and tusks were instantaneously locked together. The two beasts swayed to and fro in the centre of the arena. The bull, making a violent effort to free himself, plunged suddenly upwards, and the point of his horn entered the lower jaw of his enemy. This was, apparently, the first time that the elephant had experienced any sensation of pain, his previous wounds having been but scratches, and disregarded in the heat of combat. But now the fury of the enormous animal seemed fully aroused, and, giving forth from his tossing snout a trumpeting sound, fierce, wild, and piercing, he shook off the bull and trotted ponderously round the ring.

The panting bull, although enfeebled by exertion and dropping gore from a great gash in his chest, stood still without flinching in the path of the elephant as he approached him, butting down his long horns to receive the attack. But it was seen that the small eyes of the elephant gleamed with a red and dangerous light from beneath the broad bald brow, and, in a moment, the long proboscis, like a writhing serpent, was enfolded round the neck and head of the bull, dragging him down with a crash upon the bloody sand. The gigantic brute then fell on his knees, full upon the upturned side of his prostrate foe, who was actually crushed to death. While the ribs were still heard cracking under the weight of the elephant, the roar of the human multitude mingled fearfully with the victorious trumpeting of the vengeful monster.

The following morning we started at dawn straight across the island to the town of Artá, situated on the eastern coast, forty-five miles from Palma. We were accompanied by a guide, who had with him a supply of blue-lights, roman-candles, and other combustibles, with which the famous stalactite caves of Artá were to be lit up for our gratification. We hired a little open carriage and a couple of small, wiry horses, which carried us over the well-made road with considerable alacrity.

In the afternoon we reached Manacor, which, next to Palma, is the largest town in Majorca, having a population of about 12,600. It is a very clean town, rather glaring in appearance, from the liberal use of whitewash. In external aspect it is a cross between the Spanish and Oriental, but, otherwise, is remarkable for nothing in particular.

Late at night we arrived at the little town of Artá, and jolted over the rather undulating pavement of its streets. The sensation was by no means agreeable, though, fortunately, it was of short duration, and, therefore, was tolerated with greater patience. We slept at the smallest and most primitive of *posadas* imaginable! The style of architecture it would be impossible to determine, though the building was very simple in structure. It consisted of a heap of bricks, mortar, dried mud, whitewash, and a board or two, with little holes scooped in the edifice, helping to form the apartments. The supply of fresh air was not so deficient as usual; for in the sleeping-rooms window-frames were apparently regarded as superfluous luxuries.

After a frugal meal, we attempted to enjoy a little slumber; but it proved to be equally frugal in amount and quality. As early as it was possible for cocks to favour each other with their shrill responses, there was a perfect concert of cock-crowing around the house, and, we believe, on the top of it too. The ornithological entertainment began and was kept up with great spirit until our guide knocked at our door to go through the very unnecessary ceremony of calling us. It is true we were supposed to be enjoying our repose in a *posada*, or "place of repose," but the noises that commenced with the first dawn of morning were so numerous and so loud as effectually to murder sleep.

We started in the early morning, after a refreshing breakfast of red mud, called chocolate, some black bread, and no butter. After walking across fresh prairie lands, green with sprouting corn, and over sandy tracts interspersed with aloes and the universal olive, we began to ascend the steep pathway at the foot of the mountains covered with dark pine trees, dwarf oak, and arbutus, which led to the mouth of the cave. The cave is hewn out of a vast mass of limestone, of which the hills in this neighbourhood are composed. We toiled upwards, following the steps of our guide, who, as well as a little boy whom he had pressed into his service by the way, was laden with a perfect fagot of port-fires, blue lights, and other combustibles.

Before us was a magnificent natural arch, the vaulted roof of which rose to the height of a hundred and forty feet. By this vestibule of nature we approached the darkening galleries tunnelled in the rock, and leading to those mysterious caverns which concealed so much that was beautiful in the deep bowels of the mountains. As we advanced, the obscurity deepened, and we had to light our torches. Happening to look back, we perceived the bright archway of light at the entrance diminished into a luminous speck in the distance. Upon reaching a level space, at the foot of a rude hewn staircase, we found ourselves in the middle of a splendid hall or vaulted chamber, in which the uncertain gleam of the torch fell faintly upon tall uncouth objects, apparently white, though rather dim in hue, standing at intervals. Without any extravagant exercise of the imagination, one might have pictured to himself this chamber as the Pit of Acheron, and these gaunt shapes as the petrified forms of those doomed to imprisonment in its gloomy recesses.

The great pillars which adorn this noble hall are calcareous deposits, formed by the everlasting droppings from the percolated roof above. We picked our way further downwards over a wooden staircase, with the natural roof rising over us into arch after arch of great beauty, but irregular form. The guide, accompanied by the boy moving on in front with blazing torches, looked like some demon with his attendant imp luring us spellbound into some vast and fatal labyrinth. One great hall in which we found ourselves was noble and grand in appearance. In the middle of the gloom loomed masses of fretted white stalactite, rising upward in spiral forms, while some tall, slender objects appeared like the graceful stems of palm-trees capped with feathery plumage. These were formed by the pillars, as they joined the roof, being pushed backwards and spread out like boughs of drooping foliage.

In another chamber called the Hall of the Virgin, a marvellous effect was produced. In the middle of the spacious concave we dimly perceived some lofty object of a grey and misty hue. "Momento," said the guide, "don't move;" and in another instant a blue light was kindled. No words can describe the effect that was instantaneously produced. The walls shone like crystal of dazzling brilliancy. The roof was like a firmament ablaze with a million stars. The numerous columns that supported it were adorned with a profusion of filigree work which had some resemblance to Gothic tracery. A lofty marble-like pedestal, apparently supporting a graceful female figure which, amidst many folds of gauzy drapery of the most brilliant whiteness was caressing a sleeping infant, composed a group at once beautiful, majestic, and serene.

In the Hall of the Organ there is a great number of airy white pillarets collected in a mass, which in the gloom natural to these subterranean halls have some resemblance to the pipes of an organ. Wandering about in passages that appeared almost like aisles in nature's temple, we anticipated every moment a burst of mysterious melody in harmony with the wonderful character of a place so rarely seen by human eye.

The name of the Hall of the Curtain is sufficiently suggestive of what is to be seen in the chamber so designated. A wall of dazzling white stone is of such airy texture that it seems in the fitful glare of the torches to be driven backwards and forwards by the wind. So, in the Hall of the Banners, a flag appears to be drooping from its staff and occasionally waving in the breeze. We know it is only a delusion, but for the moment it is wonderfully like reality. As we followed our guide in these awful caverns by stairway and corridor, through hall and gallery, we could almost imagine that we were pacing the courts of some buried palace of some long-forgotten Titan race.

In a magnificent vault called the Hall of the Theatre, the tiers of boxes and rows of benches have a startling resemblance to reality. Had spectators equally ghostly in appearance dropped in one by one, or rushed forward in a mob, we could scarcely have been more amazed. The secret processes of nature, the works of unrivalled beauty which it has produced in these deep recesses, are truly marvellous beyond all conception.

As we walked about the caves we were constantly tripped in our path by what seemed to be innumerable petrified oranges cut into halves, and adhering to the ground. On inspection these turned out to be stalagmites in embryo, coagulations of the lime-droppings from the roof, from which the water had not evaporated. They are of the brightest orange colour, a hue which is due to the presence of iron in solution. By the guide they were called "poached eggs."

We bade farewell to those realms of splendour with feelings we should vainly attempt to define. Among the many objects of interest we have visited in different lands, we never saw anything that made a deeper impression on our minds than these silent galleries. Even the thought that so few of our countrymen had ever visited, or even heard of them, tended to make us explore them with more than usual interest. The recollection of the wonders of nature hidden from all the world down in the caves of Artá nothing can efface from our minds, though probably it may never be our fortune again to visit them.

We had been advised to visit the caves *usque ad nauseam*, but had paid little attention to the counsels of the local admirer. We had listened to them as the traveller does to the exaggerated accounts of the caves of Skye or Fingal given by the natives. When the caves of Artá, however, burst upon our vision, their grandeur and novelty were so startling that we were overwhelmed with astonishment and awe. When there are so many people eager after new sensations, we would ask, why, in the name of all that is beautiful, pure, and majestic, do they not go to Majorca as well as to Homburg? Access to the island is easy enough. There are two lines of steamboats to and fro—one from Valencia, the other from Barcelona. The inhabitants are civil and hospitable to a degree. The hotels, in this respect unlike those of Spain, are both clean and comfortable. The scenery, as we have shown, is so magnificent that it cannot be surpassed in Europe, and there are several places in the island of great historical interest.

FOOTNOTE:

[34] Corridas de toros.

CHAPTER XV.

CONSIDERATIONS ON SANITARY MATTERS.—THE MEDICAL PROFESSION IN SPAIN.—THE ART OF PACKING.—NIGHT SIGNALS.—EL GRAO.—CHASSE AUX CALEÇONS ROUGES.—VALENCIA.—DRIVE THROUGH THE CITY.—THE CATHEDRAL.

THROUGHOUT Spain, as we have observed, and as all travellers will notice when they visit that country, innumerable vile odours prevail everywhere and are one of the most unpleasant characteristics of the country. This, together with a general ignorance or carelessness of all household draining, of course proves one of the most fruitful causes of the cholera which periodically creates such awful ravages throughout the land. It is quite curious how callous a Spaniard appears in the midst of the most frightful odours that can be imagined. While we can scarcely breathe, being compelled to hold our noses in such a way that we are almost suffocated, the dignified Spaniard moves along as serene and untroubled as if he were amidst the rose-gardens of "Gul in her bloom." In fact, he seems rather to like odours that to others are insupportable. If his opinion coincided with that of some medical men, who consider bad smells good for health, he could not endure them with greater equanimity.

Majorca is comparatively free from this pest, although the sanitary arrangements of Palma are still very primitive. Two years ago, cholera raged furiously in the city, and on many of the doors of the houses and palaces one still sees notices which were written in chalk at the time, for the dead-cart to wait for a load as it passed through the streets—exactly as in London during the plague two hundred years ago. On the fine old doorway of the palace belonging to an English gentleman—a post-captain in the British navy—to whom we were much indebted for great kindness and hospitality tendered to us during our sojourn at Palma,—we found the following inscription scratched in chalk:—"Muertos: Juan. Lorenzo. Faustina."

Many years ago, in order to force the Spanish doctors to be more assiduous in the study of their profession, it was ordered by Government that on the door of the house of a medical man there should be traced as many red marks or crosses as the number of patients who died under his treatment. A nervous Englishman arriving in Madrid became indisposed, and sent his servant to explore the whole city in quest of a doctor who, having the fewest red marks chalked on his door, must consequently have—as he concluded—the fewest deaths to answer for. A medical gentleman was thus discovered whose residence was distinguished by only one mark, and him the Englishman immediately retained. The invalid congratulating himself before some friends on what he considered a "treasure trove," they clasped their hands, and exclaimed—"Dios! What have you done? You have chosen the worst doctor in Spain! He never had but one patient in his life, and he died under him!"

It is astonishing the horror of fresh air entertained by Spaniards. On one blazing day—the day before our departure from Palma—while we were undergoing the agonies of packing our portmanteau, an old lady rushed violently into our bedroom without "with your leave," or "by your leave," and, while giving utterance to a torrent of incoherent sounds, expressive either of remonstrance or resentment, slammed together the window-frames, the greatest anxiety being at the same time depicted on her countenance, and her eyes looking at us with a glance which seemed to say "Are you mad?"

Packing is a great art quite as much so as the comprehension of Bradshaw. In our opinion the art of packing, Bradshaw, carving, and manners should be taught at all schools as distinct branches of education, in order to render a man what Mrs. Malaprop would have called an "Admiral Crichton." It is very curious that at every place one leaves one finds that the portmanteau holds less than ever, and has become smaller in spite of having generally left something behind at the last place, until, in very despair, one simply uses very bad language, takes up all the things, and flings them *en masse* into the trunk; and then, having danced a little war-dance on the lid, sits moodily down upon the same like a perspiring Banshee on a wall, and smokes a cigarillo, or makes one's notes.

What a blessing have those men lost in these climes who bathe not, neither do they swim! The bathing is perfect at Palma, in that red-hot climate and dark blue sea. The water is warm, and to good swimmers, as buoyant as a feather-bed, with the advantage of having no fleas; though perhaps, now and then, so they say, with the little inconvenience of a stray shark or two. The length of time one may remain in the water without experiencing any chill, is remarkable. One can, in fact, lie on his back, with face upturned to the soft blue skies and almost go to sleep. Indeed, the astonishing thing seems to be how anyone can sink in this heavy medium. It is so transparent at the entrance of the Bay of Palma, that, during a calm, weeds can be distinctly seen at the depth of forty fathoms, waving at the bottom among the stones and shells.

In the Middle Ages, Majorca suffered much from the inroads of the Barbary pirates. Even now the old custom is kept up of lighting beacons every night all round the island. As soon as one is lit, the next follows until the entire circle display their signals. All remain lighted one hour after the last has been trimmed, and are then extinguished to show that the island is in perfect security.

We were sorry when the time for our departure from Majorca arrived. As we left its shores, we looked back with regret on the bright villages nestling amongst the orange groves and olive lands. We felt sad when the pretty city of Palma, with its towers, terraces, and cathedral, was hidden for ever by a projecting headland. Our gaze lingered with a melancholy feeling on the Great Dragonera Rock, with its flaming beacon—the westernmost point of Majorca—and on those mountain peaks with which we had become so familiar, as they melted away into the warm haze of the Mediterranean.

"On the wide waste of waters was no living thing,

Save the vanishing gleam of the sea-bird's white wing."

And the Evening Star looked down on the wave like the eye of the mariner's guardian angel. The night was calm and balmy, scarce a breath disturbed the surface of the waters, and enwrapped in a Valencian *manta*, we lay down to rest under the clear firmament, and were lulled to sleep by the Arabic drone of the man at the wheel.

The early rays of the dawn as we awoke were lying warm on the white walls of a place with which we were familiar, the port of El Grao, and lighting up the distant towers and spires of Valencia. El Grao, with its flat-roofed eastern houses, and its long line of white meeting the blue sea below, together with the lofty lateen sails of its shipping, and the palm-trees fringing the coast, might have been, as far as appearance went, some Syrian port.

I was again compelled to incur the pity and contempt of the good Spaniards by getting into a boat to do a little natation before landing. I excited their astonishment, if not wrath, by climbing out of the water up the side of a vessel at anchor, for the purpose of taking a header from its bowsprit. On the sudden appearance of my naked form and red *caleçons* upon the deck, the mariners at once came to the conclusion that I was either a maniac or an Englishman, an idea which emboldened them so much that they chased me from one end of the ship to the other, uttering loud cries. The *chasse aux caleçons rouges*, however, soon came to an end; for on arriving at the figure-head of the vessel, I simply disappeared, head foremost, overboard, to the undisguised amazement of my pursuers. On rising to the surface I saw seven men, and a marine with fixed bayonet, staring dumbly at me over the bulwarks. "Addios, Señores," cried I, and swam off to my friend in the boat, who also had been sporting like a dolphin in the deep while taking his bath.

In Valencia cows' milk is as great a luxury as ginger-beer in Yucatan. The milk of goats and mares is the staple commodity—that of cows, when it is to be procured, being advertised about the town on placards at a heavy price to tempt the rich, in the same manner as one sees rare wines announced in London. In fact, to the common herd of mortals, Spain is not a land flowing with milk and butter. Oil, however, is universal, being found in cakes, in pastry, in soup, in fact in every dish, betraying its presence even in the very air itself.

Amongst the rules of etiquette in vogue with the lower classes in Spain, is the custom of offering you a mouthful of whatever they may be eating while you are holding intercourse with them. We are happy to add, however, that it is equally the custom to refuse. It is bad enough to have to astonish our organs of digestion by eating all the strange compounds we do eat at *la mesa redonda*, or *table d'hôte*, in the hotels of Spain. What a doom must it be for a member of the Reform Club to travel for a few weeks in the Peninsula! The very idea would make Soyer turn in agony in his tomb in that country whose stomach he left his native land on purpose to benefit.

After landing at El Grao from our swim, we again jumped into the "taratana," and once more were bumping through the dust, stones, and ruts of that ridiculously bad road under the acacias, towards the pest-house hotel, where we supposed the one-eyed beggars would be awaiting us, not only on the stairs, but at the very doors of our bedrooms. On we went through the green avenue, past the battalions of red-legged, white-capped soldiery, drilling on the broiling sand and under a vertical sun. We crossed the yellow bridge of the Guadalaviar, with the statues of virgin and saint with tin hats on their marble brows. Again we were in the midst of the long, dark, cool streets, in which resounded the clanging of church bells, and looking up at houses behind the coloured awnings and blinds of which dark, laughing, wicked eyes gleam like those of snakes from the obscurity within the half-curtained windows. We rode quickly past the arabesque buildings, the rich Gothic churches, the sculptured palaces, and the Moorish courts, through the gaudy, noisy market-place, with its stirring crowd, in garb as bright and various as that of a harlequinade, and out into the blazing white squares and sunny gardens, until the cool dim vault of the old cathedral once more hung over us like a grey cloud of stone.

In the interior of the cathedral are hung the spurs and horse-bit of the Cid. When Valencia was conquered from the Moor, those pieces of rusty iron were placed there by the hero's hand hundreds of years ago, and remain till now as witnesses of his immortal chivalry. He died in Valencia in 1099.

Within the old cathedral are noble classic arches composed of rare and various marbles. Lofty Corinthian columns support magnificent domes, from the coloured windows of which the sun-rays stream upon the curling smoke of incense which, rising in circling clouds, gradually disappears in the immense arched vault above. The choir, so richly adorned with carved oak, is filled with crimson-clad priests, attended by dark-eyed boys swinging silver censers, and bearing aloft great flaming candles. Besides the display of wonderful carving and gilding, there are brazen railings of the finest workmanship, a multitude of gems of dazzling brightness, and figures of the Virgin Mother and Christ arrayed in robes of unexampled magnificence—altogether such a display of ecclesiastical wealth as is seen nowhere but in Spain in these modern days. On the walls are portraits of saints and paintings of scenes from sacred history, most of them, if not all, works of great value.

In strange contrast to the wealth of the church are the crowds of beggars crawling in an unutterable state along the marble pavements, on which all sorts of foul abomination are allowed to lie for days. In the midst of this ecclesiastical splendour, the altars are specially to be noted for the wealth that has been expended on them, and for the beauty of their design. But from these we turn to the arches and pillars of stone which carry us back to that remote era, darkened by ages, when the church was founded. The organ too is evidently a noble instrument, as we can judge by the fine tones which it emits while accompanying the monotonous chaunt of the priests. The rich coloured glass of the windows gives such variety to the hue of the light which it admits, as to add very much to the solemn impression produced by so magnificent a temple.

We climbed up to the summit of the cathedral tower, panting in the hot air and dust, and amidst those sour unpleasant odours which seem to be a *sine quâ non* with all the interiors of Spanish and Italian churches, not excepting the towers. If these are the odours of sanctity of which we hear so much, they are certainly far from agreeable. Arrived on the summit of the old lofty yellow belfry, from which a beautiful young woman had thrown herself for love a week before, a view of fairy beauty was spread out before us. Beneath lay the city with all its domes, towers, and pinnacles, its fantastic architecture, its gloomy Moorish gateways, and its piles of Saracenic ruin towering in melancholy grandeur, like ghosts of departed power, amidst the downfall of all their pride.

There lay the green gardens, gleaming with marble fountains and statues. The houses are of every hue. Noble mansions are flecked all over with white lace-like arabesque decorations. Spacious squares and teeming market-place are seen amid the confusion of the labyrinthine streets, rendered sombre and cool by their overhanging eaves, almost apparently touching each other, and thus shading the winding way below from the burning rays of the sun. Away in the distance, all around the yellow walls of the city, are fruitful plains, with here and there masses of deep green foliage streaked with the grey of the olive. From north, west, and south, a noble amphitheatre of purpling mountains surrounds the city. In all directions orange groves, with their golden burden, and shrubs of gaudy hue, give a rich appearance to the land. The splendid chestnut and the tall palm-tree wave their branches, fanned by the warm and scented air. Sparkling villas, slender spires, and sunny villages, scattered far and near, are shining in the midst of the green and smiling plain, while afar off, bright, broad, blue, and beautiful, appears the hushed and trembling sea. Truly nowhere is a nobler view to be seen than that around Valencia, the fairest of Mediterranean cities.

CHAPTER XVI.

DEPARTURE FROM VALENCIA.—A RAILWAY JOURNEY.—DIFFICULTIES TO WHICH TRAVELLERS ARE EXPOSED.—TARRAGONA.—SKETCHES OF ITS HISTORY.—ARRIVAL AT BARCELONA.

WE departed from Valencia, regretting to quit so soon a city where there was so much that was attractive. The train moved off, and after we had proceeded a short distance the night came on. Our appetites being sharpened by long fast and the sea air, we inquired of the guard at which station the passengers would descend to dine. Being told at Castellon, we leant back on the cushions, smiling at each other with that benevolent expression of countenance which the prospect of the refreshment of the inner man produces on the outer—a sort of artificial good-nature, in fact. So fickle, however, is the mental constitution of man, so evanescent everything appertaining to human nature, that in about an hour from the happy moment just recorded we were sitting in extreme and opposite corners of the carriage, addressing *staccato* remarks to each other, which, although intended to be general, and to carry with them all the *suaviter in modo* required by the conventionalisms of good society, were at the same time remarkable for the transparency of their tenor. And though in our conduct to each other we had been perfect models of outward politeness, the manner and tone of the conversation became somehow painfully civil, not to say rather nervous and unpleasant, like that of two persons who, having at length, as they think, found each other out, adopt a tone of studied high-polite reserve, not unmixed with a complacent consciousness of their own superiority. And why all this? Wherefore this sudden estrangement between two fond hearts? The answer is simply Stomach, and nothing more; for it is trying, very trying, after one has been assured that dinner waits at a certain station, to find upon arriving there, mad with hunger, that no adequate preparation has been made for you, and, on asking for the *buffet*, to be directed to a greasy board in the open air, behind some wooden palings, presided over by a dirty old man with two saucers before him full of snails, a plate of minnows, and a collection of little cakes made with rancid oil instead of butter, which condiments we have to clutch at through the railings like monkeys in a cage, the only light being the illumination afforded by a farthing candle. We say it is very difficult under such circumstances to avoid the display of a little ill-nature.

The railway from Valencia, going somewhere in the direction of Barcelona, is a miserable mockery of civilisation. The engine one would imagine was about five-horse power, by the pace at which it went; and it had to stop every five or six miles to renew its supply of water. To all appearance it was simply an old boiler, furnished in a hurry with a few mechanical intestines. Not the least of its evils was that it emitted a pestilential black fume. The motion of the train had an effect upon the passengers something analogous, we should think, to that of being tossed in a blanket.

At a dreary broken-down village called Amplora, at eleven at night, in pitch darkness and drizzling rain, the Barcelona railway came to an end. We were aroused from a feverish sort of sleep by the light of a strong lantern turned full upon our faces. Having undoubled, and stretched ourselves out from a sort of patent boot-jack position, we were hastily packed up tightly, like figs in a drum, with a snuff-coloured gentleman, and stowed away within the fragrant recesses of the *coupé* of what was confidently supposed by the misguided natives of those regions to be a *diligence*. With our heads touching the ceiling of the *coupé*, and knees protruding through the front windows, while our luggage, boxes, parcels, and cloaks were thrown on the top of us, as if they had been heaped there with a pitch-fork, we found ourselves, it need scarcely be remarked, in a very uncomfortable position. It was not long before a collision took place between us and the Moorish-looking gentleman, our companion, whose chief characteristics appeared to be a profuse abuse of snuff, unchanged clothes, an unwashed skin, and an eagle eye. He said he was unwell, and had been told to avoid fresh air. The Anglo-Saxons said they also were unwell, but as a renewal of the oxygen in the atmosphere was considered beneficial to health, they had been advised to avail themselves of the fresh air as much as possible. We were pressed so tightly into our seats, that we looked like owls in an ivy bush, except that those luckier birds rarely have several hundredweights of luggage piled upon their bodies, so as to leave only their heads visible inside a Spanish *diligence*. We do not suppose either that the owls, which are generally considered partial to the fresh night air, would much like travelling with a gentleman who preferred to be cooped up during his journeys in an exhausted receiver. We were actually packed like preserved sprats in a barrel, and the Moor, who had grumbled until he could grumble no more, was seized with a violent fit of shivering and sneezing, which on the whole was very creditably played by him, and might have established for him a second-rate notoriety in low comedy at a minor theatre. He caught hold of all the rugs and cloaks he could lay hands upon, and, utterly careless of the proprietorship of the same, built a wall thereof between himself and the deadly open windows on our side of the *coupé*, and so subsided into a sort of angry slumber, broken by constant snorts and groans.

Off we started, the rays of the lantern on the front of the *diligence* above us streaming ahead on a team of eight white horses, and into the darkness beyond. There were two coachmen sitting on a bench immediately in front of us, considerably blocking up the small windows. These two individuals cracked their whips in a wonderful manner, until they almost played tunes therewith, giving tongue at the same time to a long duet of curious howls. Having thus relieved their feelings, they again cracked their long whips over their heads, making the eight white horses dash away amidst a peal of the little bells which were suspended all round them. On we rushed at a furious pace through the darkness, and through thick clouds of dust, rolling whitely upwards through the glare of the lamp. We passed a straggling collection of weird old trees, which nodded like passing ghosts, and disappeared in the gloom. With the earliest streaks of dawn, wild-looking mountains, dark and distant, arose in all directions, and great rocks, dilapidated villages, and mournful plains, dotted here and there by a solitary figure in uncouth garb, came in turn into the focus of the lamp. Now we swept round a sharp corner, and saw the eight white horses curving round after each other, apparently far off in the misty light, and the two coachmen, muffled up in their great shaggy coats, sitting side by side like a couple of brown bears erect on their hind quarters. We rattled and jumbled with a noise like that of near artillery over a gaunt wooden bridge, piled all over with stark black scaffolding, while the light of the lamp streamed in blood-red streaks on the dark flowing waters beneath. A group of unearthly-looking buildings on the opposite shore then came into view, hazy, indistinct, and undefined; and after passing under a high stone arch, we found ourselves in a long dark street. On each side were windows with black blinds, and the ghostly walls, reared high above us, seemed as if about to fall in ruins, and bury us in a mass of stones and rubbish. As we rattled on with a deafening noise, we turned the angle of a large edifice which looked like a mouldy fortress of other days. From the number of houses around us we must have been passing through some town or city; but no sign of life, human or animal, save ourselves, intruded upon the solitude; and night and loneliness reigned heavily over all. We at length passed with a succession of violent jerks over a crazy, neglected-looking drawbridge, and through some huge ramparts, and left the city behind us, with its deep black river flowing on in the silence. We hastened at a lively pace over brown open plains, encircled by jagged iron-like mountains, which, at first looming in the distant dawn, soon received us into their bosom. In a short space of time the jangle of bells diminished, while the whips exploded into a farewell fantasia. The drivers or coachmen climbed down from their perch, and in a moment more we descended, heated, dusty, wearied, and fretful at the miserable barn-like railway station of Amposta, where we found a *table d'hôte* which groaned beneath the weight of a dish of olives, a plate of dissected cock, some salad, and a bottle of wine, remarkably *ordinaire*, which a shilling bottle of port from a Whitechapel gin-palace would have put to the blush. There were also some jovial viands in the shape of filthy little globules called grapes, and a few sour flabby turnip-like vegetables entitled apples. Truly travellers often see strange things in this country, to be remembered, of course, among the *cosas de España*.

Here we got into a hot railway box, stuffed with cushions, apparently filled with oil, from the odour they emitted, and then jogged along at the rate of about six miles an hour. We were thankful to be well clear of that depressing place, Amposta, and sat quietly in the carriage, dreamily inhaling the morning air as we glided along. The stars were gradually disappearing from the vault of night, or paling in the advancing glory of the coming sun. A few golden bands flamed across the eastern heaven, heralding the sun's first kiss on the morning of a new day.

In a short time we were coasting along the Mediterranean waters. Now we crossed a fragile looking wooden bridge, and swept high over the waves which gently broke beneath. Then a lovely view of blue curving shores with rocks and light-houses, and of the smooth sea flecked by the white sails of numerous feluccas, broke upon the sight. Our road, however, turned suddenly away from the coast, and we proceeded inland through hot sandy plains, and occasional orchards of orange, citron, and pomegranate. Groups of white flat-roofed houses gleaming in the sun, with the palm trees waving over them, were seen pitched amongst green fields of long bamboo, Indian corn, rice, and tobacco. Sometimes we were near enough to rugged-looking mountains, to descry the dwarf oak and arbutus with which they were clothed in all directions.

Tarragona was the next town we reached. Close to it we saw great aloes, many of which were sprouting from the sand and rock-strewn beach, and from the prostrate masonry of the Cæsars. There are two towns, the higher and the lower, which are separated by a line of walls. The higher city sits majestic on a lofty rock of limestone, and from a height of eight hundred feet looks down upon the azure sea. The houses are mainly composed of the ruins of Roman palaces,—even the simple home of the artizan is adorned with marble friezes, or upheld by portions of Corinthian columns;—and on the white marble flags in the courts of the Imperial Baths, the swine were basking in the sun.

The climate of Tarragona is now, as it ever was, mild and genial, and the summer heat is tempered by the cool breeze of the sea. So salubrious was its air held to be, that the Roman Prætors always established here their winter quarters, and Tarragona became the capital of Roman Spain. It was originally colonised by the Carthaginians, and the flower of its youth were enlisted to swell the armies of the great enemy of Rome. Publius and Cneius Scipio, however, occupied the city, and compelled it to submit to the Roman sway. Tarragona, in the war between Cæsar and Pompey, declared for the latter, but upon his defeat at Pharsalia, humbly submitted to the conqueror, and Julius resided within its walls, calling the city "Julia Victrix." Augustus Cæsar passed one winter here, B.C. 26, and the ruins of the palace where he dwelt may still be seen supporting some ignoble bricks of modern Spain.

Tarragona stands amidst the fallen splendour of ancient Rome, while the stern mountains rising darkly around, though comparatively changeless themselves, look down upon the scene below, which, amid the wreck of an empire, speaks so eloquently of the uncertainty of human greatness.

We had just congratulated ourselves in having got rid of the Moorish-looking gentleman who had been constantly afraid of catching cold from an open window behind his wall of packages in the diligence, when we were favoured with the society of another native gentleman who had already caught cold, and, like all his countrymen, was terribly afraid of fresh air. As the sun increased in power our friend seemed to decrease in caloric, and proceeded at length to encase his legs in a sack, at the bottom of which was a hot bottle. When one of us approached the windows he requested that they might be kept well closed, in order "to preserve our atmosphere;" but unfortunately we could hit upon no expedient by which we might "preserve *our* atmosphere" without destroying his at the same time, and so the eternal *quæstio vexata* of fresh air had to be argued once more.

The new acquisition was at first very taciturn. As the day, however, became perfectly broiling, and the hot bottle began to do its work, he seemed to show signs of thawing a little, and some of the ideas that had been ice-locked within his mind during the night began to dribble out before the warmth of day. He, however, knew as little of English as we of Spanish. For example, in explaining that we thought night-travelling a great bore, we were astonished to hear him say that—"Zee voyage in zee noctes was 'a great male pig.'" He had, of course, on some occasion looked out in the dictionary for "bore," and turning to "boar" by mistake, had found the explanation, "Boar—male pig," a piece of information which he had fondly cherished in his mind ever since, to display at the first opportunity, as a proof of his linguistical acquirements.

After a weary time, as we rattled along the iron way—the *ferrocarril*, as they call the railroad in Spain—the white town of Barcelona began to come into view, with its handsome outlying villas and its busy manufactories, all glowing in the bright sun, in the midst of fruitful olives and gigantic aloes. When we had reached the Station, the ever-wakeful *aduanero* was there to welcome us in his own peculiar way. A smile, a joke, the offer of a cigarette, and the title of *Señor* to the dirty functionary, produced the usual satisfactory effects, and we were dismissed with a polite salute before even the Inspector arrived. Without the loss of a moment's time, we were seated on the knifeboard of an omnibus, which immediately began to wend its way through the pretty boulevards of the city, and amidst the gay houses flaunting with bright blinds and awnings, which look down on a beautiful double line of plane trees forming a grateful avenue in the midst.

The Fonda de las Cuatro Naciones is a charming hotel in every respect, perhaps the best in Spain. Several of our countrymen had taken up their quarters here before us, and, according to custom, had made themselves remarkable by what we may call, if not the usual, at least the travelling peculiarities of the Briton *en voyage*. In the streets of Barcelona we again came across the Britisher prowling about as usual, looking very shy and miserable, the expression of his countenance seeming to say that he would be very grateful to any one who would tell him what to do with himself. Why is it that so many Englishmen creep about foreign towns as if they were ashamed of themselves—as if they were anxious to avoid the human eye, or had committed some awful crime?

CHAPTER XVII.

BARCELONA.—HISTORICAL REMINISCENCES.—CASTLE OF MONJUICH.—THE CATHEDRAL.—THE GRAND OPERA.—THE PLAZA DE TOROS.—THE LITTLE ROPE-WALKER.—MONTSERRAT.

BARCELONA, once the rival of Venice, and now the chief sea-port of Spain, seems to be a bright, clean, and prosperous city. Its aspect, so far at least as regards its principal thoroughfares, is that of a feeble imitation of Paris. Its streets in general are as bad specimens of paving as are to be found in the Peninsula. The only truly national thing about the place is the odours, which we must regard as essential properties of a Spanish town. The long-suffering traveller's nose must resign itself with the best grace possible to the incessant inhalation of that variety of oleaginous and ammoniac smells which to Spaniards, we suppose, must be among the necessities of existence. There are few Moorish remains, as the Moors held Barcelona only for the comparatively short space of eighty-eight years, being expelled in 801 by Charlemagne, who added the city to his duchy of Aquitaine. The wise and the curious have determined amongst themselves that Barcelona was founded by Hamilcar the Carthaginian, who was also called Barca (*Anglice*, thunderbolt). However, it is quite certain that Augustus Cæsar raised it to considerable importance, making it a *colonia* under the appellation of Julia Augusta, Pia, Faventia, and the rest. During the Middle Ages, Barcelona was the centre of learning and the resort of troubadours. Columbus was there received by the Catholic king to whom he had given a world. In 1543, steam was first applied to ships of 200 tons at Barcelona by Blasco de Garay; but from certain political complications and rivalries the experiment, though successful, was discouraged. Of course we had the constant pleasure of meeting, "whene'er we took our walks abroad," our old friends the sunburnt cigarette-smoking beggars, who with Maffeo Orsini cried, "*Il cigaretto per esser felice!*" Black with sun-burn, dirt, and age, having apparently nothing on earth to do, and plenty of time to do it, with lots of people to help them, they lounged about the portals of those wonderful churches one meets with so often in Italy and Spain—church, barn, and fortress lumped together, as if the building had not yet made up its mind what order of architecture it wanted to belong to—to what purpose, temporal or sacred, it was to be devoted.

"*Donde el mar?*" cried we, on descending from the knifeboard.

"*Par ici, M'sieu*, coom vid me, *va bene*—all right;" and away we go with the commissionnaire, having provided ourselves with towels, to the boats, and in a quarter of an hour were lying on our backs on the dark blue wave, as on a sofa, looking up at the great brown isolated hill of Monjuich, with its fortress crest rising eight hundred feet sheer out of the sea, turning our eyes to the forest of masts in the distant harbour, regarding with interest the white sparkling town, its domes, towers, and wharves roaring with busy life, backed in the distance by clusters of purple mountains, or curiously watching the sea-gulls, as with their white pinions they wavered slowly in the soft warm blue air above us. This was luxury. The French say the English do not understand *luxe*. Ignorance is a voluntary misfortune, and it is a pity that our censors don't see to it.

The red-capped, lazy, brown, one-eyed old boatman was much astonished at the fact that any human beings could be so mad as to enjoy a dip in the sea in such a glorious climate. When he had so far overcome his surprise as to be able to row us back to shore, we flew on the wings of hunger to a breakfast of fresh sardines, cutlets, quails, figs, and amontillado, the interval between each dish being occupied by smoking a cigarillo, *à la manière Espagnole*.

By the way, in order to illustrate the carelessness, timidity, obstinacy, malice, or whatever flaw it may be in the Barcelonese boatman's character, I may observe that, having placed great confidence in the fact of my having a boat ready to follow me in my swimming excursion, I quietly swam in this delightful blue, warm, and buoyant water about a mile out to sea, never dreaming but that the boatman would follow. Upon turning round, however, with a view of re-entering the boat, I descried it, to my amazement, about a quarter of a mile astern, and in it two human beings, apparently engaged in fierce dispute, gesticulating violently and waving about their arms. These were the boatman and my friend, who had just emerged himself from his bath. The latter naturally wished the boat to follow me, in case of any sudden current carrying me away to seaward, but the boatman distinctly objected to that proceeding, remarking, "Me no go, Engleeshman out dare too mosh wash!" meaning, "This friend of yours out there has swam out too far for me to care about following him, so now he will have to come back by himself, for I shall go no farther." However, the oars were soon in the stalwart hands of my friend, and in a few minutes the boat was alongside of the Englishman who had "too mosh washed" himself.

Thus refreshed, we could now enjoy a stroll in the town. The day was beautiful, the sun shining brilliantly. And so onwards through the shady boulevards and the cool narrow streets, in which we mingled with a half-bred sort of French provincial capital population. The fine mule, with its gaudy trappings, is not frequent here; and all such Spanish sights as picturesque, dirty men in old velvet hats, sashes, coloured blankets, and sandals, are, alas! as rare as ortolans in Tottenham-court Road. In the course of our walk we came to the town gates, and emerging from them, found ourselves on a white road, glaring beneath the rays of an African sun, the heat insupportable, and the dust insufferable. Picking our way among stones and aloes, we began the ascent of Monjuich, the name of which is derived from *Mons Jovis*—a temple dedicated to Jupiter having been built upon the summit of this mountain by the Romans.

From the fortress cresting the mountain is seen the entire town of Barcelona lying below, with the harbour and its crowd of shipping gay with the flags of every nation. On the southern side is spread out a wide tract of pestilential marshes, seething in the sun, and yet occupied by a number of human habitations. Fever, it need scarcely be said, rages throughout these regions the greatest part of the year. Only those who are compelled by the hardest necessity live and work in such an unhealthy locality. It is painful to think that in a scene so attractive, where nature clothes herself in some of her most beautiful forms, sickness and death should strike down so many victims. To the west, the sunny slopes of the distant mountains are seen gradually lessening in the far haze, until they appear to be lost in the sea. The castle of Monjuich is a most important stronghold, and in case of revolution, invaluable to those in possession of it, its guns commanding the entire town.

Barcelona is the second largest town in Spain, and the most prosperous and flourishing in a mercantile point of view. Its marts, quays, and ware-houses are strongly built, and the general aspect of this Manchester of Spanish Lancashire is busy, thriving, and cheerful. Connected with the Atlantic ports by railways, and with the world by the sea, upon which it is so charmingly situated, Barcelona, with its industrious, bold, intelligent, and good-natured population, should allow no rival to supersede it in the arts of commerce. The climate of its winter is bright, mild, and even. Snow is seldom seen, and the average number of days in which rain falls is but sixty-nine out of the 365. The heat of summer is no doubt great, but it is tempered by the Mediterranean breezes. In the country around the city, the plains are covered with orange and pomegranate groves, and the hill sides are variegated with the pretty country seats, or *torres*, which so enraptured Washington Irving.

It must be confessed, however, that it is rather disappointing to find so little of the real Spanish element in so large a town of Spain. Valladolid and Barcelona are alike, inasmuch as they both possess arcades; but where one is intensely Spanish, the other is terribly Lowtherian, and recalls Burlingtonian memories. The system of begging seems, too, to be carried on here in a very refined manner. In one of the most frequented *plazas* in the city, we were, on one occasion, suddenly accosted by an elderly lady covered with a quantity of black lace, and otherwise dressed with great care and propriety. Upon taking off our hats to inquire what service we could have the happiness of rendering her—thinking, perhaps, that she might be ill and wished us to call a *fiacre*, or still better, that she was going to ask us to dinner—she simply demanded a few reals "for the love of God and Saint James."

During the recent revolution a few urchins, either from mischief or from the design of their dupers, shouted one day upon the public promenade, when at its fullest, the words *Viva Prim!* Instantly the over-zealous gendarmes on duty pointed their carbines in the direction from whence issued the cry, and a flight of bullets was sent among the terrified groups of people in the streets. Several perfectly innocent persons, including two ladies and an infant, were mortally wounded. The knowledge of this melancholy fact, which had occurred only recently, did not make it more pleasant to us during the hours which we spent daily in the society of a Spanish gentleman who had taken a fancy to us. Being a violent democrat and of a most impulsive disposition, he was in the constant habit of talking in a dangerously free manner, in a painfully loud and distinct tone of voice, about the above-named general, bringing out the word "Prim" so sharply and distinctly that we really expected, every time he uttered it, to experience the sensation of being riddled with balls and slugs from any point of the compass. As we repeatedly urged upon our "dear friend," we did not in the least care who was who, or what was what. It was a matter of no concern to us that in Spain the wrong men were in the wrong places—the square men in the round holes, and the round men in the square holes—nor would it cause us the slightest uneasiness if they remained there till Doomsday. All this we took the greatest pains to impress upon our acquaintance, especially after hearing the before-mentioned anecdote; but still, at disagreeably short intervals, the word PRIM, ever and anon, rang out with startling distinctness, causing us as much uneasiness as we should have felt if we had every moment expected the explosion of a shell at our sides.

The cathedral, of course, had to be *done*; and it is wonderful how instinctively the tourist hunts out his natural mental food unaided. In Italy, after breakfast, at any new place, it is always "Now for the *Duomo*!" And so in Spain, in spite of the intricate windings of streets and general labyrinthine state of the towns, sure as the trained hunter upon his quarry, does the tourist seek out and find his *chasse café*—the cathedral. Well, perhaps, there is nothing on earth more sublime, majestic, and imposing than one of those masterpieces of Christian architecture, a Spanish cathedral, no temple more fit and worthy for the worship of the Eternal.

The Cathedral of Barcelona, like many others in Spain, is built upon the site of a Moorish mosque, and is magnificent in design, though the impression which it produces is perhaps rather sombre. Darkened chapels, dimly lit with twinkling lights, throw out a subdued blaze of splendour from their gorgeous *retablos* and glinting brazen railings. Above, the glorious Gothic arches meet in all their florid beauty, like the trees in some heavenly avenue. Long rows of stalls and seats—miracles of wood-carving, surmounted with spiry pinnacles of the darkest oak, whose wondrous tracery seems like a canopy of heavy lace spread upon them—surround the choir. Bare marbles gem the walls, the air is stained with rich and solemn colouring from the gorgeous windows, and the fragrant smoke of incense rolls in slow grey clouds around the ancient columns.

The Royal Opera-house of Barcelona is one of the largest in the world, and when it is filled has a most enchanting aspect. As the Barcelonese are particularly partial to amusements, and, in fact, to all kinds of gaiety, they have acquired such taste in self-decoration and personal adornment, that a very fine general effect is produced when the great *salle* is packed to overflowing with the *beau monde*. At this opera-house one sees a perfect galaxy of dark, and, we may say, blazing beauty; for amidst the rich silks, the gorgeous satins, and the gay ribbons of all colours, brilliant with sparkling jewels, there shines out from every female face the yet brighter jewelry of large Spanish eyes flashing the quick emotions of the human soul as the music falls, stirring like a breeze, upon its chords. The number of uniforms, too, glowing from all parts of the great theatre, render the scene very gorgeous; and the manner in which the glittering multitude occasionally rises excitedly *en masse* to applaud and wave their kerchiefs, as they spontaneously feel the sudden effect of some passage of unusual power, is perfectly electric.

The performance, however, compared with that witnessed at Madrid, and still more with that of the London or Paris Operas, was, when we were at Barcelona, tame and mediocre. The whole company seemed more or less in a general state of chronic melancholy and chromatic scales. Roderigo chiefly relied upon his legs and one high note, and was continually poising himself on one of his feet like a zephyr beginning his training. Why, we wonder, are all Othellos on the lyric stage in a general state of perspiration? And when a gentleman in an opera wants to curse his daughter, why does he invariably dress himself in black velvet and imitation point lace, while the lady herself must appear with her back hair down? It certainly is very curious, though quite Spanish, to observe, in about four minutes after the descent of the curtain at the end of each act, the entire opera-house filled with the smoke of tobacco, and one experiences a novel sensation when, walking on the grand staircase, he stops to light his cigarillo at one of the gilded lamps. It is of little use for English ladies to complain of tobacco in Spain, and it is questionable taste in them to be indignant, as we have seen many, on finding themselves involved in clouds of smoke. Besides which, all mankind have to bear their burdens in one way or another, and the fragrant scent of the Havannah leaf is surely a trial light enough to endure amongst the greater trials of life. Men have to tolerate women in their *vapours*, why should women not make the same allowance for men during theirs? Each nation, like each individual, has its idiosyncrasy, and the great maxim, "What can't be cured must be endured," ought never to be forgotten by travellers, especially those who are strangers to the customs of the country in which they are temporarily sojourning.

The Plaza de los Toros, or Bull Ring, situated in the *quartier* called Barceloneta, where the poorer and labouring classes, together with a community of ship-chandlers, reside, has no pretensions in appearance to anything else than what it is, namely, a great wooden slaughter-house. When we arrived in the city the bull fights were over for the season, and the ring was used as a circus and gymnasium for acrobats and athletes. We witnessed within it, however, a spectacle, bloodless indeed, but still with the scent and thirst of blood—and human blood, too—about it, which we may hope can scarcely be witnessed in any other civilised land, whose fiercer passions are not kept in a chronic state of ferment by festive shows of wanton cruelty, and whose tender youth are not deadened from the dawn of their sensibilities to all love of mercy and sympathy for suffering. A female child of seven years was brought into the great arena, which was covered with human beings, their faces all turned upwards. She was engaged to walk the entire length of a rope inclined from the floor on one side of the building up to the roof on the other, about a hundred feet in height. Upon taking her place on the rope, just before commencing her perilous journey, the poor child, suddenly seized with a panic, burst into tears, and evidently shaking with fear, implored to be excused. At this sight, the helpless child trembling in sight of her death, it might be, what emotions filled the breast of the great crowd? Sorrow for young innocence in deadly peril for the idle amusement of the spectators? An imperative desire to rush forward and rescue that tender child from wanton destruction? Did any mother's heart, fluttering with loving thoughts of her own infant, yearn for the rescue of this poor little being, tricked out in sparkling tinsel and pink gauze, trembling alone in mid air on a single rope? No! they all thought only of the value of their miserable pence, and loud rough voices were heard in all directions execrating the child. "Push her on—make her go," they cried, and shook their fists at the poor little creature, whose tears now rained down her cheeks as she looked from side to side, imploringly for one friendly glance. But there was none. With a sudden impulse, however—apparently of pride—she shook her head defiantly, gulped down a sob, and grasping the balancing pole, started on her high and narrow path. She arrived, thank God, at her destination safe and sound, not only, however, without a note of approval or applause, but amidst hisses and jeers. This certainly was a painful page in the study of a nation's characteristics, without one redeeming trait to soften the painful effect it produced, it is to be hoped, on many minds.

Near Barcelona is Montserrat, the *Mons Serratus* of the Romans. Upon a wild and rugged mountain, hewn and carved into a weird distorted mass by the mysterious forces of nature, is pitched a monastery. The view from the summit is, of course, magnificent, and the innumerable grottoes with which the great serrated mountain is honeycombed, are as usual very dark, damp, fatiguing, and unwholesome. Though no doubt they are curious and wonderful, one is apt, after having done a certain amount of grottoes and stalactite caverns in various parts of the world, to say, when the words "How marvellous!" are dinned into the ear, "We wish to goodness it was impossible!" as Dr. Johnson observed when he was listening to some celebrated performer on the fiddle. The blunt lexicographer, who was no respecter of persons, was, however, possibly right, for, when flatterers meet, Satan goes to dinner—there is no need for him to stay, in fact; those whom he leaves behind him will do all the work for him.

The railway from Barcelona to Gerona passes through a succession of lovely landscapes. The traveller is carried past lofty chains of hills clothed up to their summits in the deep green of the waving pine. The iron road then passes through sweet valleys, the gentle floors of which, smiling in the sunshine, are covered with the richest verdure. Occasionally the eminences which crown these valleys are crested with the broken masonry of other days; as we journey onwards—castles, forts, old ramparts, crumbling walls, rear up in all directions like skeletons of the past. When the scene begins to show signs of human habitation, we pass white villas and farm-houses, terraced round and hung with balconies, over which grow luxuriant creepers. Solitary mansions are sometimes seen gleaming out from the dark verdure of the woods, or sitting on the velvet surface of ample plains. Then the railway carries us past the channels of dried-up rivers, and over stony plains, which appear to stretch away until, in the distant horizon, they meet the soft blue line of the Mediterranean. There we enjoyed from a considerable distance our last few glimpses of those fairy waters, with many a white lateen sail resting upon them, like the weary wings of some exhausted sea-bird.

CHAPTER XVIII.

ANCIENT BRIDGE OF GERONA.—THE POPULATION.—A FIESTA.—SEARCH FOR AN HOTEL.—THE FONDA DE LA ESTRELLA.—LAST SIEGE OF GERONA.—THE CATHEDRAL.—A FEW CONCLUDING WORDS ON SPAIN.

WHEN at last the train stopped in the outskirts of Gerona, we mounted on the top of an omnibus and were whirled off through a boulevard of plane trees, in which were groups of very *plain* folk, who—it being a *fiesta* day—were dancing and whooping in large circles in a frenzied manner that to us calm onlookers was very remarkable. The sight, however, was brilliant and animating. Scarlet caps, red sashes, velvet breeches, and jackets covered with flashing metal buttons, together with the brilliant petticoats and embroidered bodices of the females, produced a scene that was altogether of the most lively description.

Upon emerging from the avenue of plane trees, the town of Gerona burst suddenly upon us. A wonderful old town it is! Talk about the picturesque! Where are all the artists who frequent Wales, Margate, Scarbro', and the over-done East, who give us perennial views of the same, *usque ad nauseam*, until people need never have moved out of London to know them as well as the inhabitants of those places themselves? Why don't they travel hither, and put before the jaded British public this intensely interesting and most extraordinary place? Here they may find novelty and variety to please the most exacting taste. The city as a whole is very old and quaint. Rickety houses appear sometimes to be piled up indiscriminately upon heaps of gaunt battlements and crumbling ramparts. The brown decaying walls tell many a story of the violence and lawlessness of other times. The people of the present day live in houses which are built of the remains of old forts, and are constructed of anything that came to hand at the moment. Rocks, stones, wood, dirt-heaps, mud, old bricks, old ruins, rubbish, all have been raked together, and piled up confusedly into habitations; and a most unique, heterogeneous, and dangerous mass they seem. Houses and other buildings bend and bow to one another in all directions in a very stiff and awkward manner, as if the whole place had been suddenly paralysed in the midst of some general act of politeness. One edifice props up another, as the lame support the lame. There is one church, indeed, constructed out of some old convent walls of great solidity, that supports four feeble houses which lean bodily upon it, and without it would inevitably fall down like so many card-houses. It requires some judgment to walk about with security in the interior of many of these charming dwellings, the strange old rooms necessitating great steadiness of gait and correct judgment of eye, for the floors are not always so level as one might desire. There are heights and hollows which it is advisable to avoid as much as possible if one would escape painful bruises.

Gerona is in reality one of the quaintest and most ruinous cities of Spain. When its population are not dancing war-dances in the streets, it is very desolate and silent. It is entirely without trade or manufactures; and, barring its beautiful tiful Catalonian cathedral, it is without any worthy monuments whatever, and has nothing to attract the attention of the least exacting of tourists. It is supposed to have been founded by the tribe of Bracati Celts, as far back as the year 930 before the Christian era; and from the earliest times up to the French attack in 1809, it has again and again been battered, knocked about, and almost depopulated by repeated sieges, while its inhabitants, when any were left, have been decimated by famine and disease. Like a phœnix, however, the old city has risen again from its ashes. As it stands now, it is constructed entirely of ruins. The home of squalor, and priests, and decay, it is appropriately built upon the vestiges of the past. The little river Oña winds its serpentine course through rows of crazy houses, covered all over with wooden balconies filled with flower-pots, and gay with coloured rags. The houses seem toppling and pitching towards each other over the dirty stream, which is spanned by a picturesque old three-arch bridge, also in a most ruinous condition.

Where the citadel crumbled before the French cannon of 1809, there is now a high heap of rubbish bish, on the top of which are perched groups of eccentric-looking houses, built of the shattered bricks and *débris* hastily raked together, and piled anyhow into something resembling human habitations, with a noble disregard of all design, and apparently even of the laws of gravity. The town is all up hill and down hill, full of holes, ditches, and dykes. The arcades are mouldering; the courts dark and malodorous; and where there are flights of stone stairs, they are old and broken. There are churches and convents, but they are old and out of repair; there are forts, but they are battered; and battlements, but they are crumbling. A young fresh-looking child in such a place would appear an anachronism; but there are plenty of the most repulsive-looking beggars. A total absence of all sanitary arrangements causes the atmosphere of the town to be actually felt as well as smelt. A greasy mist seems to envelop it. Yet poor as Gerona is, what heroism has from time to time been displayed by the gallant inhabitants!

As we have said, we arrived on a *fiesta* day—a Sunday, and found all the young men in the town—for such there are in it—collected in the squares and courts, and walking round and round in rings, or pacing hand in hand to a measured cadence of song, something like that of howling dervishes, and looking very solemn, silly, and hot. This indeed seemed a most limited idea of amusement.

Heaven defend us from the hotels! Our diligence stopped at one. We got down to inspect it, and, on advancing, were immediately swallowed up by a dark archway leading to unknown depths beyond, and vomiting in our faces one of those volleys of terrible smells which are indigenous. Retreating in dismay, we took, as a matter of conscience, one glance up at the front of the house, and one look into it. We could imagine what the whole would be—a series of winding passages leading to whitewashed, uncomfortable rooms, with windows without glass, but grated and barred. Lean-eyed fowls, mostly moulting, would probably be roosting on the hat-pegs in bedrooms, while the floors would present a liberal collection of magnificent specimens of the pale-pink cockroach. Presiding over all this, no doubt there would be a greasy creature in the shape of a landlord, looking at us as if he had the Evil Eye, and wanted to give us a taste of its power. Seeing this would never do, we made one bound into the interior of the diligence, and hid ourselves, with quaking hearts, amongst some warm old ladies, with their bundles and umbrellas. At the next hotel we found a Spanish gentleman, our companion in the train from Barcelona, who had been so civil as to offer us a gold cigarette case as a present, which, unfortunately, we were told etiquette compelled us to refuse. What a waste of time that sort of thing is!—as absurd as two men going out to fight a duel, and snapping off copper caps at each other. However, there he was, leaning over the balcony of the Fonda de la Estrella. *Étoile*—Star!—The Star and Garter? No, most distinctly *not* The Star and Garter.

Our friend, as we have said, was leaning over the balcony, gratefully inhaling the dismal smells which arose from the street below. As he had taken rooms for us, we went in, determined to remain, though we could see presages of what our fate was to be. Our friend had laid himself down, and covered himself with a rug, to go through the farce of taking a little rest, but after he had, by a strong effort of imagination, supposed he had refreshed himself by his siesta, we looked upon his countenance as he arose, with the rug still upon him, and saw that it resembled a magnified pepper castor more than a human visage. All the mosquitoes, fleas, and flies in Gerona must have concentrated their forces upon his face, and held thereon perfect orgies for a couple of hours. The hotel altogether was a very miserable establishment, not more inviting than the preceding one.

After we had retired to rest, the floor creaked in a very uneasy manner throughout the live-long night. The walls of our sleeping apartments were painted black, and every article of furniture was preserved from the disastrous effects of damp by the time-honoured dust of ages. Moisture was continually dropping from the ceiling on to the floor below, with a sound as regular as that of a slow pendulum. In an apartment where sleep is generally uncertain, the counting of these drops, and their arrangement into minutes, quarters, and hours, might prove a very pleasing pastime. We dined, on the evening of our arrival, most luxuriously on stewed beef made of *Plaza de Toros* horse, and suffered severely from cholera and cramp, in consequence, for three days after.

In May, 1809, the French, with 35,000 men under Verier and Augereau, besieged Gerona, and it was not till after seven months and five days' fierce and incessant struggle that the indomitable inhabitants, unable to hold out longer against famine and pestilence, were compelled to yield. Forty French batteries were in position, but the gallant Geronese, with guns of inferior caliber and metal, but mad with hatred to the foreigner—their religious enthusiasm at the same time being fanned to the most desperate pitch by the priesthood—fought with the despairing energy of fanatics. Women served and loaded the cannon, and lay dead everywhere by the side of their husbands and brothers.

The first sentiment experienced by the Geronese as they saw from their walls the advancing host of the French was not that of terror, but a burning desire for revenge, an unconquerable feeling of hatred towards the spoilers of their hearths and homes, which made them welcome the coming combat as they would a religious *fiesta* or popular ceremony. The women laboured unweariedly at the fortifications with pick and spade, joining with the men in the most arduous duties; tearing their delicate hands as they piled the great rough stones and tugged at the clumsy cannon, and cheerfully bending their frail forms beneath the weight of heavy burdens, they encouraged with look, gesture, and smile the men of Gerona, the soldiers of a day. All those who could carry a weapon seized it, and praying the priest to bless it, kissed it as a precious gift of heaven. Young and old, strong and frail, rushed with enthusiastic shouts to man the walls, determined to do or die. Not a creature was there but thirsted for the combat, the heart of all beating with one glorious pulse. Rich and poor knew no distinction: all were equal in their love of God and country.

Nor did the actual terrors of the fight diminish the spirit of valour with which they had commenced it. The dead, as they fell, were blessed by the watchful priest, and envied by the survivors as martyrs. As the siege progressed, another and more fearful foe appeared in their very midst, against which the mightiest could not prevail. The dead fought against the living; for the accumulated corpses of the slain, few of whom they were able to bury, brought a pestilence upon the town. Still the heroic defenders fought on unflinching, and fell down rotting at their guns. Then arose a cry for bread, for pale-eyed famine hovered over the city. All the domestic animals—the faithful friends and slaves of man—had been pitilessly slaughtered and their flesh eagerly devoured. Even the rats of the river had served as nutriment to the garrison, and the dead themselves at length supplied Gerona with a ghastly but imperative food. Still amidst blood and slaughter, amongst the wildest horrors of plague, famine, and war, Gerona held out against the foe, until, after seven months and five days of iron determination and indomitable courage, it fell exhausted, crushed, and prostrate into the hands of the enemy. Fifteen thousand men had perished on the side of the French, and nine thousand on that of the Spaniards. Thus ended the last siege of Gerona; and as long as true patriotism and unflinching courage excite our warmest sympathy, the names of Saragossa and Gerona should be watch-words to all true lovers of their country.

We went to the theatre at Gerona, which we found to be a large, painted apartment, reeking with the odour of tobacco. The drama of the evening was rather complicated in structure, and must have been harrowing in incident, judging by the effect it had on the spectators. The plot was so absurdly incredible as scarcely to deserve mention. The hero was discovered by his father to have married his step-mother. The unfortunate gentleman, whose wife had married his son, perambulated the stage in apparent distraction, every now and then stopping at the wing to have his tears renewed by a wet sponge. The dialogue must have been magnificent, to judge by the number of ahs! and ohs! to which the audience gave vent. As far as the actors were concerned, it was perfectly unnecessary, as the prompter did it all for them, in a very audible manner. Indeed, at times, so distinct, clear, and forcible was his reading of the play, that the leading tragedian was not only perfectly inaudible, but became utterly speechless, contenting himself with "sawing the air," and doing a little dumb-show, ever and anon taking a few measured paces. The prompter himself, at any passage requiring extra force, jumped up in his little shed in front of the footlights and waved his arms aloft like railway signals, and then as suddenly disappeared.

When every one in the tragedy was disposed of by death, the curtain fell, and we walked back to our hotel with an energetic little Spaniard, who kindly accosted us, telling us he was very impressionable, and at the sight of an Englishman could never restrain himself from tendering to him his respect for the British generally, and for Sir Gladstone in particular. He certainly was one of the most voluble individuals we ever had the misfortune to come across. He told us all he knew upon every subject, and a great deal besides about which he knew nothing; ending by informing us that he had a great admiration for everything noble and grand, an assurance which he finished by swindling us in the easiest manner possible out of the sum of five shillings—English money.

Before the traveller takes leave of charming old Gerona—and, in spite of its many discomforts, to leave it one is loth—let him wander once more through its quaint old rickety streets by twilight, and note the dark serrated broken sky-lines of its houses. Wandering on, he will come suddenly upon the beautiful ancient cathedral church, with its imposing lines. It is a truly magnificent edifice, and one cannot look up to its lofty arches, so sombre in their aspect, without being impressed by the gloomy majesty of this old Gothic temple. Through its splendid brazen gates the eye catches the gleam of twinkling tapers casting their rays upon groups of gaudy priests, while all around them, amid the white curling cloudlets of ascending incense, falls the halo of soft light, in which they appear as in a vision. Dark shrouded figures, scattered over the marble floor, apparently motionless in prayer, were kneeling before the altars or amongst the ancient tombs. An organ of great power was pealing forth one of those magnificent pieces of music which the Romish Church has dedicated to the service of religion; and, at a distant altar, a splendidly robed priest was reciting some of the services of the Church. Who, whatever his creed, could remain unmoved in such a fane?

We are now at the end of our ramble, but before we return to the delights of home, we may as well add a few words of plain fact concerning the once all-powerful and still illustrious Spain.

The chief characteristics of Spain appear to be oil, dirt, priests, and bull-fights; for, without these, Church and State possibly might not cohere. Spain is a congeries of contradictions. It is very cold, and very hot; very beautiful, very ugly; very fruitful, very barren. The mental character of its population is simply a counterpart of the physical nature of the country, and is doubtless almost entirely influenced by climatic peculiarities. The Spaniard is distinguished by much natural sharpness of thought and acute intelligence. A serene and gentle spirit is often found amongst them, and they are generally extremely courteous to strangers who tread their soil and are within their gates.

The Spaniard possesses a very ardent imagination, and his passions are often very excitable—sometimes even uncontrollable. The continuous insurrections which distress the land give evidence of the constant state of fermentation in which the spirits of the population are steeped. A certain amount, however, of physical languor, engendered by the heat of their climate, and descending to them from old Saracenic blood, is blended with great mental activity and an impassioned nature. In their ordinary actions they are often gentle in the extreme, but when their passions are awakened they not unfrequently become ferocious. Calm, yet fiery; indolent, yet energetic; revengeful, yet affable; enthusiastic, yet morose; avaricious, yet generous; but, above all, superstitious and narrow—such seems to be the Spanish character.

Yet how lamentable it is to notice a country so richly endowed, whether in human talent or in natural blessings, and once the most powerful kingdom of earth, now so fallen and degraded, descending to the lowest shifts and chicanery; so utterly without influence or respect; so backward in civilization and morality, political and social, amongst the nations of Europe! In fact, Spain is—or very recently was—a dead country, whose monuments and morals are alike in ruins. Native industry is unappreciated, and foreign talent taxed to extortion. The Spaniard can rarely be roused to exertion, beyond those periodical attempts to subvert vert a bad government by the exile or slaughter of hundreds of honest and innocent people. In matters of importance he too often follows that mistaken policy which always hugs delay, and cries, "*Mañana*," to-morrow, always to-morrow. To-morrow comes, but Spain, the Spain of Charles V.—like the Rome and Greece of old—is no more; and, in the present slough of reckless indolence, bigotry, jealousy, isolation, internal dissensions, and utter lack of all homogeneous force, we fear, notwithstanding the more hopeful circumstances of the present, can never return. There are great minds and honest hearts within the country still, but an unkind fate has ordained that they should remain powerless, that place-hunters, parasites, and favourites may reign supreme, beneath the ægis of a despotic government, which is directed, barring that of modern Rome, by the most uncompromising of all the Catholic priesthood. As the enemies of civilization, honesty, and common sense, Rome and Spain may go arm-in-arm, the scorn of all nations, the distrust even of themselves, and a disgrace to the nineteenth century. Jesuits, monks, police, and spies, are the order of the day; while the press is gagged or servile, and all liberty of thought strangled like a dangerous snake.

Spain is a splendid territory, rich in Nature's wealth, but poor indeed in those attributes which alone truly elevate a nation—viz., a general firmness of character, desire of progress, love of liberty, purity of administration, and power of action. In Spain there exists no art, no science, but what is borrowed with bad grace from other countries. Literature, which once struggled for life, is now utterly prostrate. Its death dates back to the Inquisition, to that religious community who exercised all their holy zeal to kill the body and suffocate the mind. If there is absolute truth in Socrates' conception, that all human aspiration and effort should be generally directed towards the acquisition of knowledge, then surely are the Spaniards of to-day most aimless in their existence. In fact, the influence of the bigoted Middle Ages, when, with relentless severity, heresy was suspected in everything said, written, or done, was sufficient to destroy the taste for literature, had Spain even possessed a literary community. Philosophy or science can make no progress where reason fears to dwell.

Certainly, Cardinal Ximenes, one of Spain's most enlightened men, struck with shame at the continued ignorance and mental darkness in which the priesthood were sunk, had the courage lent him by his station and loftier mind to found the University of Alcala de Henares at the commencement of the sixteenth century. He revised the cramped version of the Scriptures, substituting for it a rendering more adapted for intellectual acceptance by compiling at his own expense the famous Complutensian Polyglot, although crushing, at the instance of the Holy Office, all attempts to translate the Bible into the Spanish tongue. He also made a yet greater step in the advance of intellectual liberty by inculcating the law which excludes Papal bulls not sanctioned by the monarch. In spite, however, of this considerable improvement in the education of the ecclesiastical mind, notwithstanding this attempt at cleaning a portion of the Augean stables of darkness and superstition, the long chronic hatred entertained, by the Executive, of all liberty of thought, and their love of power, had become too engrained a habit to allow of much more being done in one lifetime than to temper it with the seeds of a possible improvement, and merely to insert the wedge of tolerance. All that could be tortured by the cunning of partial priests into the merest suspicion of heresy, in speech or in writing, was still punished with incarceration, confiscation, torments, and death, even by the sanction of this Cardinal patron of letters himself. Under these circumstances, literature of any other sort than that of romance, mysticism, or biographies of saints, now found but dangerous ground to take root; for wherever the author was, there were the priestly supervisors gathered together. Surely the birth of culture and enlightenment appears but in the funeral train of superstition.